ALIAS BILLY THE KID

ALIAS BILLY THE KID

C.L. SONNICHSEN
AND
WILLIAM V. MORRISON

CREATIVE TEXTS PUBLISHERS
Barto, Pennsylvania

ALIAS BILLY THE KID
C.L. SONNICHSEN
WILLIAM V. MORRISON

Published by Creative Texts Publishers, LLC
PO Box 50
Barto, PA 19504
www.creativetexts.com

ISBN: 978-0-692-53404-5

To
Melinda Allison Roberts—
gentle, steadfast, and loyal

TABLE OF CONTENTS

FOREWORD FROM THE 1955 EDITION

Some years ago, a Southwestern writer stated the case for Brushy Bill Roberts (and for this book) in the following manner:

Was Billy the Kid really shot to death by Sheriff Pat Garrett on that July night in 1881, or was someone else the victim? Nose in and out of some of the tiny Spanish-American villages of eastern New Mexico and seek out the old-timers, gray and bent with age. They will shrug their shoulders and lift their hands and answer, "*Quien sabe*? Who knows?"

The rumors have persisted about many men, good and bad; men whose lives have refused to be contained between two dates on a tombstone; men who "came back to life" once, twice, or several times- to the consternation and utter disapproval of the historians and keepers of vital statistics; to the delight of the romanticists, the folklorists, the writers, and the readers of popular legend. These stories have been published many times, in fiction and non-fiction.

Marshall Ney, listed in the history books as having been executed for treason in France in 1815, is said to have lived out a pleasant old age near Raleigh, North Carolina. Oscar Wilde, John Wilkes Booth, Jesse James, and many other famous or notorious men have claimed- or had claimed for them- one or several physical reincarnations. These are phenomena of literary, if not historical stature.

So, Brushy Bill Roberts is not alone in his claim to have survived a death historically credited to him. He is, if not unique, at least one of the very few such claimants whose claims have been subjected to careful, expert, extensive examination while he was still living.

We, as Southwestern regional publishers, feel this way about this book; It is interesting. It is a new facet of the perennial Billy the Kid legend. It contributes new material to that legend- new facts, new interpretations, and new contradictions. We believe that it is the product of honest research that the facts presented as facts are facts, whether or not they support the claims based on them. On these grounds, if none other, we believe that this book merits publication.

It will not convince the skeptics- yet even the most skeptical readers of the manuscript have been amazed by what Brushy Bill knew: things never printed; things even in contradiction to the accepted stories, since proved to have been the way Brushy Bill told them. (It was generally believed, for example, that there was a federal charge outstanding against Billy the Kid. Brushy Bill said the case was "thrown out of court." The legal records, when found, proved Brushy Bill's statement.)

If you are an addict of the Billy the Kid legend, this book will cause you to think hard over what you think you know about it, if only for purposes of argument, pro or con. Whether you know or care about the Billy the Kid legend or not, you will find here an interesting story in an established literary tradition: the story of a man who laid claim to a legend.

AUTHOR'S NOTE TO THE SKEPTICAL

THE TALE which follows will seem simply unbelievable. Even to those who believe with some readiness, the story of Brushy Bill Roberts will not appear fantastic enough. But, surely anybody, skeptic or not, will agree that it is a curious piece of human experience, and that it deserves to be recorded. For Bill Roberts claimed to be Billy the Kid. He declared that Pat Garrett's bullet killed another man in Pete Maxwell's yard that night in July, 1881, and gave a detailed and circumstantial account to support his claim.

The intention of this book is to let Brushy Bill tell his own story, without addition or subtraction, and to throw as much light on it as possible by citing newspaper accounts, correspondence, eye-witness testimony, and official records. No attempt is made to highlight, select, or color Bill's statements. His editors, one a lawyer and the other a college professor, are probably more than ordinarily respectful of sources, verification, and evidence. They would not willingly participate in a deception. They have set down only what they can vouch for, and have not attempted to draw final conclusions. So far as they are concerned, Brushy Bill stands on his own feet.

They have no intention of attacking anybody, living or dead, and ask only for a patient and understanding hearing of an extraordinary story.

Many old- and new-timers have helped in putting the book together, so many that not everyone to whom thanks are due can be named. Mrs. Melinda Allison Roberts, Brushy Bill's widow, should have first mention. She did everything she could to help. Robert N. Mullin, of Chicago, Illinois; Clark Wright, of El Paso, Texas; and Mrs. O.L. Shipman, of El Paso, have read all or part of the manuscript and given of their deep knowledge of Western history and tradition.

The late Oscar Garrett, of Odessa, Texas (son of Pat Garrett), and Colonel Maurice Garland Fulton, of Roswell, New Mexico (foremost authority on the history of southern New Mexico), talked freely about the case, though neither of them took any stock in Brushy Bill's account.

George Fitzpatrick, editor of the New Mexico Magazine, contributed valuable material from his files.

The late Noah H. Rose, of San Antonio, supplied unique photographs and an invaluable friendship.

The names of the men and women who assisted by correspondence or by signing affidavits appear in their proper places and need not be mentioned here, though they too deserve hearty acknowledgement.

Others who have helped include the following: R.F. Roberts, of Beaumont, Texas; Henry G. Morris, of St. Louis, Missouri; Ted Andress, of El Paso, Texas; and H.R. Parsons, of Fort Sumner, New Mexico- all attorneys; the late Albert H. Clancy, former United States Attorney, Santa Fe, New Mexico; Joe Martinez, Attorney General of New Mexico, Sante Fe; Alicia Romero, former Secretary of State for New Mexico; Cecil W. Williams, County Clerk, Fort Sumner, New Mexico; Carmen Armijo, Deputy District Clerk, Las Vegas, New Mexico; J.G. Moore, County Clerk, Carrizozo, New Mexico; Mrs. Geraldine Mathisen, District Clerk, Las Cruces, New Mexico; Beatrice B. Roach, Secretary of State, Santa Fe; Ernest Key, Carrizozo (for assistance with the court records); A.S. Gaylord, Jr. , formerly librarian, the Museum of New Mexico; Mrs. Helen Farrington, Erin Humphrey, and the staff of the El Paso Public Library; Margaret Irby, former librarian of the New Mexico Military Institute, Roswell; Caroline Dunn, Librarian of the Indiana Historical Society, Indianapolis; William J. Hooten and Bill Latham, of the El Paso Times; Hawley Richeson, El Paso Chamber of Commerce; Mary Nell Taeger Brown, of Denison, Texas (formerly of the Ruidoso News, Ruidoso, New Mexico); E. A. Brininstool, Los Angeles, Calif.; Ernest S. Pollock, Silver City, New Mexico; Jim Kimbrel, of Picacho, New Mexico (son of Sheriff George Kimbrel); James S. Guyer, Bangs, Texas; R. K. Stone, of El Paso (for making photographic reproductions); and Mrs. Erlwood von Clausewitz, of El Paso (for help with the manuscript).

C.L. SONNICHSEN
WILLIAM V. MORRISON
El Paso, Texas, March 10, 1955

PROLOGUE

IT WAS about seven o'clock in the morning when Bill Morrison and his elderly friend, Brushy Bill Roberts, walked into the restaurant to get breakfast. Morrison saw the headlines on the front page of the Albuquerque Tribune as he passed the cashier's desk. He had the paper in his hand as they sat down, and the more he read, the less he felt interested in food. "GOVERNOR MABRY TO INTERVIEW BILLY THE KID CLAIMANT," the story said.

"The chat is the result of a recent request from an El Paso legal firm that the Governor pardon their client, who claims he is the notorious desperado."

It was the next paragraph which took away Morrison's appetite.

"Several historians have been invited by Mabry to attend the interview. One is W. A. Keleher of Albuquerque who takes a definite stand for the story Garrett killed Billy. Others are Paul A. Walter of Santa Fe and Will Robinson of Albequerque.

"Also invited is Wilbur Coe of Clencoe. He is the son of Frank Coe, who with his brother George took part in the Lincoln County War, in which the Kid figured prominently. Frank and George Coe are dead.

"Mabry said the El Paso law firm said it did not want its client "molested" by reporters, but the Governor said reporters would not be barred from the meeting and could question the aged man after the official interview.

"Meanwhile, Radio Station KGGM in Albuquerque suggested the Governor, rather than pardoning the Kid, if the old man proves to be the famous desperado, should insist that he face trial. Billy had a murder charge hanging over him."

"What's the matter, ain't you hungry?" Roberts asked, already chomping away at his breakfast.

"No," said Morrison. "I don't believe I'll eat till after this interview is over."

Over the long-distance telephone in Ted Andress' law office back in El Paso, Morrison had told the governor that he would introduce his man if the conference could be private. Roberts was afraid- afraid of being hanged or, at least, of being trapped somehow. He would go if he could see the governor alone. Not otherwise. There was no telling what might happen now.

At this moment the ancient warrior seemed unworried. He had dressed for the part he had to play- the big hat with "Brushy Bill" on the front of the leather sweat band- the red silk handkerchief around his neck (he loved red things)- the fringed buckskin jacket with the horseshoe-shaped trim around the pockets- blue jeans- shiny cowboy boots. He looked many years younger than the ninety-one years he claimed, and seemed steady enough.

Well, they would have to go on now and take things as they came. The stopped at La Fonda hotel, in Santa Fe, to call the governor and let him know they had arrived. Morrison was politely indignant about the way the interview was being handled, and Mabry was apologetic.

"I had to give them a statement," he said, "but I told them I was to see your man at ten. You come to my house early and I'll give you a private conference, as I promised. I'll let you in the back door about 9:40."

They dodged the reporters and photographers, who were already bunched at the front of the governor's mansion, and were admitted at the kitchen door. Mabry met them as they stepped into the central hallway and greeted them cordially, but they could not fail to notice that a good many people were assembled in the front room at the end of the hall, including two uniformed state policemen, with pistols on their hips.

Roberts surveyed the assembled multitude and began to go a little shaky. "Step in here," said Mabry, and took him in to the governor's study, where there was a place to lie down. For twenty minutes they conferred behind a closed door.

ROBERTS AT THE GOVERNOR'S MANSION

The chain of events which brought Brushy Bill Roberts to that conversation in the governor's mansion in Santa Fe, on November 29th, 1950, was weird enough. It began in Florida in 1948 with a man named William V. Morrison, who was working as an investigator for a legal firm. Morrison was a graduate lawyer with a good nose for evidence, an earnest collector of odd bits of fact from bygone days, and a member in good standing of the Missouri Historical Society. He was delighted when it fell to his lot to handle a case for an old man who went under the name of Joe Hines. Joe had never thought of reassuming the name he was born with until a brother died in North Dakota, leaving some property behind. In order to get his share, Joe had to establish his real identity and Morrison was assigned to work up the documents.

It turned out that he was a survivor of the Lincoln County War, in the seventies, and had fought against Billy the Kid.

Morrison himself was a direct descendant of Ferdinand Maxwell, brother of the famous Lucien Bonaparte Maxwell, and had some information about New Mexican history. He mentioned the fact that Billy the Kid had worked for the Maxwells and added that Billy had been killed in Pete Maxwell's house on July 14, 1881.

"Garrett did not kill the Kid on July 14, 1881, or any other time," said Hines with great emphasis. "Billy was still living somewhere in Texas last year. The reason I know is that a friend of mine, now living in California, stops over to visit with me here every summer. He and Billy and me are the only warriors left of the old Lincoln County bunch."

Morrison tried to find out who this old man was, but Joe Hines would never tell his name. However, another old-timer came along who knew all the parties concerned. This was an ancient Missourian named Dalton, who already had startled the country by declaring that he was Jesse James. Dalton knew the whereabouts of the man Joe Hines said was Billy the Kid, and Morrison got his directions without waiting for the annual visit of the mysterious Californian. A correspondence began between him and O.L. (Brushy Bill) Roberts, of Hamilton, Texas, and a finally, in June of 1949, he went out for an interview.

He located Roberts in an unpretentious part of his little county-seat town and made notes on his first impression.

"When I stepped to the door of his home, he greeted me wearing a sleeveless sweat shirt, blue jeans, and cowboy boots. I was amazed to see a man ninety years old in excellent physical condition, stranding as straight as an arrow. He was about five feet eight inches tall and weighed about 165 pounds. He was smiling, blue-gray eyes dancing into my eyes, with right hand outstretched for a very firm handshake. I noticed that he had a small, neat hand with well-shaped fingers, unusually large wrist, heavy forearm, and well developed biceps. His shoulders were heavy, square, and shapely. His thinning gray hair had dark streaks running through it. He had a high forehead, prominent nose, and large ears, the left ear protruding noticeable farther from the head than the right ear. He seemed to be a happy, sympathetic, warm-hearted man, but unusually alert."

They went inside, and Morrison met Mrs. Roberts. In her presence he remarked that it was difficult for him to believe that he was talking to Billy the Kid.

The old man turned red and replied, "Oh no, you've got me all wrong. Billy the Kid is my half-brother. He is still living down in Old Mexico."

So they talked about the half-brother, and Morrison let it be known that he might make a trip to Mexico for an interview. Roberts drove back with him to his hotel and arranged for another talk the next morning. "I have much more to tell you if we can talk alone," he said.

Early next morning he sent Mrs. Roberts off to visit a neighbor. When he and Morrison were by themselves, he pointed his left forefinger at the lawyer and said, "Well, you've got your man. You don't need to look any farther. I'm Billy the Kid. But don't tell anyone. My wife does not know who I am. She thinks my half-brother is Billy the Kid, but he died in Kentucky many years ago.

"I want a pardon before saying anything about this matter. I don't want to kill anyone any more, but I'm not going to hang."

He became excited as he talked, and tears began to course down his lined cheeks.

"I done wrong like everyone else did in those days. I have lived a good life since I left New Mexico. I have been a useful citizen. I want to die a free man. I do not want to die like Garrett and the rest of them, by the gun. I have been hiding so long and they have been telling so many lies about me that I want to get everything straightened out before I die. I can do it with some help. The good Lord left me here for a purpose and I know why he did. Now will you help me out of this mess?"

"I'll help you," Morrison answered, "if you can prove to me that you are Billy the Kid. I don't believe you are old enough."

"I have taken good care of myself all my life. I do not drink of ruse tobacco. I was never drunk in my life. Of course I did drink a little when I was young, but I figured that a drunken man could not take care of himself. Some of my boys were heavy drinkers. I never had any trouble with them, though. They minded me when we were in tight places."

"Well," Morrison said, "there's one way to tell, Peel off that sweat shirt and those pants and let me look you over."

Without a word of protest the old man did as he was told and stood there in his boots and nothing else. Morrison noted his fine firm muscles. "All right, what do you want," he said.

"Tell me about that mark on your right hip."

"That scare was from the time I run into the street at Lincoln to take the guns off the body of Sheriff Bill Brady. Billy Matthews ran behind an adobe wall and fired. His shot went through the flesh of this hip and then hit Wayte. I was not hurt, but Wayte was laid up a few days.

CLIPPED THROUGH THE LEG
Fred Wayte, who sided Billy the Kid when Sheriff Brady was killed.

"Here's one I never took out. You can feel it right here. The slug entered just inside my left knee, doing downward and lodging in my calf muscle. I got it in a fight in a mountain pass northwest of Tularosa, where we sold them stolen cattle to that man."

Morrison figured out that he meant Pat Coughlan, of the Three Rivers ranch.

"The toughest battle in my life was at the Maxwell house that night. Garrett and his posse could see me out there in the moonlit yard, but I could not see them in the shadow of the house. One of their bullets struck here in my lower jaw, taking out a tooth as it passed through my mouth."

He displayed a depression in his jaw- he had no teeth and had never worn a denture.

"When I turned to jump over the yard fence, a bullet hit here in the back of my left shoulder, making this scar. Put your finger in there. After I got over the fence I stopped to fire back at them, and another of their bullets hit me across the top of my head, about an inch and a half back of the forehead, and made this scar. That was the shot that knocked me out."

Morrison added up twenty-six scars from bullets and knives. One crossed the back of his right hand just behind the knuckles, and there was another across the first joint of the trigger finger on the same hand.

"I emptied this one in a fight once," he explained, patting his left hip, "and had to draw the right one. I wasn't as fast with my right hand as I was with the left. I could fire the pistol with both hands. I fired the Winchester and both pistols from the hip. My left hand was never hit because the man never lived who could beat me to the draw with that left. I wore my pistols in the scabbard with the butts toward the back. I fanned the hammer at times. I have been ambidextrous all my life, but I am left handed naturally."

"What about the story that you could pull your hands through a pair of handcuffs?" Morrison asked.

Bill laid his thumbs inside his palms and held out his hands. The big wrists merged into the small hands without a bulge. "Did you ever see anybody else could do that?" he demanded.

Morrison said he hadn't.

He made note, among other things, that Bill wore a size seven boot; that he was thirty-eight inches in the waist, with small hips; that his chest measured forty inches; and that he wore a size seven hat.

They talked for six continuous hours, going over all the events of those far-off times and finally arriving at the trial in Mesilla, New Mexico, where Billy the Kid was convicted, on circumstantial evidence, of the murder of Sheriff Brady on the main street of Lincoln, and sentenced to hang. Brushy Bill complained bitterly, and with more tears, that the trial was unfair, that subpoenas were never served on his witnesses, that Governor Wallace had let him down by failing to come forward with a pardon as he had promised.

"But they didn't hang me, they didn't! He concluded. "I wasn't born to hang."

Before leaving for Beaumont to report at his headquarters, Morrison made an agreement with Roberts that he would arrange an interview with the head of his firm, Mr. R.F. Roberts; that Morrison himself would work up the records for the case; that nothing would be disclosed until a pardon was obtained-no pardon, no disclosure of the old man's identity. Mrs. Roberts was not to know what was going on.

On August 16, Morrison came to Hico, Texas, where Roberts and his wife had moved, and the two of them set off on a jaunt through Texas and New Mexico, intending to go over the ground where Billy the Kid had ranged and to get copies of papers necessary for carrying out their purpose. Roberts reminisced as they traveled, dredging up many a hitherto-unrecorded fact from his memories. He made mistakes and contradicted himself sometimes. He was "still running," as Morrison puts it, and dodged questions which were too pointed. He was never easy in his mind about what he was getting ready to do, but he went ahead anyway, talked to people who might have helpful information, and even submitted to having his picture taken alongside his own grave.

"They think they've got me there, buried like an outlaw with my feet to the west," he growled on this occasion, "but that won't get it. They didn't get me yet, they didn't."

He looked at the graves of O'Folliard and Bowdre and went on:

"They shot down O'Folliard like a dog in the night. They shot Bowdre down like a dog at sunup a few days later. Neither one of them had a chance. Bowdre was wearing a large hat like mine when he stepped out the door that morning. Without saying a word they shot him down, thinking he was Billy the Kid. It was not my time to go, I guess. I never was afraid to die like a man fighting, but I did not want to be shot down like a dog without a chance to fight back. They knew that I was not afraid to die, and they knew that some of them would do down with me. I always hoped I would not die by the gun, nor be hanged with a rope. I wasn't born to be hanged, I wasn't. I want a pardon so I can die a free man. I wasn't no outlaw. I never robbed banks or stagecoaches."

Morrison took the old man home and moved to El Paso to be near the records he would have to use. By the summer of 1950, he thought he had enough evidence. Since he was not a member of the bar, he went to the firm of Andress, Lipscomb, and Peticolas, of El Paso, and convinced them that he had something to go on. With their help, he got together a brief to present to the governor of New Meixo.

The contentions they sought to establish were as follows:

That Billy the Kid had voluntarily surrendered to Sheriff Kimbrel in 1879 and had received a promise that, in return for his testimony in the case of the murder of lawyer Houston Chapman at Lincoln, he would be pardoned in the event that his own trial resulted in a conviction.

That Billy had carried out his part of the agreement to the letter.

That General Wallace had only partially fulfilled his part, failing to come to the rescue when Billy was convicted and sentenced at Old Mesilla for the murder of Sheriff William Brady.

That Billy the Kid was not killed by Pat Garrett and had now reappeared.

And that it had now become the duty of the present governor to carry out the terms of the original agreement, entered into by Lew Wallace, to pardon this man and restore him to good standing in the state.

And that was how Brushy Bill Roberts came to be lying on a bed in the governor's study in Santa Fe that November morning in 1950. As things turned out, he might just as well have stayed at home.

When the private interview was over, Governor Mabry brought him out and took him into the dining room. They both sat at the big round table, Bill nearest the door. The two state policemen took up stations on either side of the entrance. The rest of the visitors stood around the walls about twenty men in all, every one skeptical of the old man's claim, though they treated him courteously.

Pat Garrett's sons Oscar and Jarvis were there, indignant about the whole proceeding. Near them stood Cliff McKinney, son of the Kip McKinney who came to Fort Sumner with Garrett and Poe the night Billy supposedly was shot. There, too, was Arcadio Brady, grandson of Sheriff Brady, for whose murder Billy was condemned to hang. Others included Will Robinson, the Albuquerque historian, and General Patrick Hurley. One at a time they turned their batteries on Ollie L. Roberts, of Hico, Texas, alias Brushy Bill Roberts, alias Rattlesnake Bill, alias the Texas Kid, alias the Hugo Kid, alias William Antrim, alias William Bonney, alias Billy the Kid.

Roberts made a poor showing. He couldn't remember Pat Garrett's name. He couldn't remember the places they asked him about. When Will Robinson asked him if he killed Bell and Olinger when he escaped from the Lincoln jail, he said he didn't do any shooting- he just got on his horse and rode off. He watched the policemen at the door and was upset when the governor pointed out one of the guests as the sheriff from Carlsbad.

The only point he scored was making Will Robinson admit that he was pretty hazy himself about things that happened sixty years ago.

When Oscar Garrett was asked to take his turn, he answered:

"I do not wish to dignify this claim with any questions."

Probably everyone at the conference was convinced that Roberts was an impostor. That may explain why no one commented on the size of his hands and wrists or asked him to show any of his scars- why there was no question about any of his physical peculiarities except the present whereabouts of his famous buck teeth.

The carefully prepared brief which had been sent to the governor was not brought out for examination and apparently had never been given thoughtful consideration by anyone in the room.

When it was over, the governor said he would defer his decision for the moment, and Roberts asked to lie down again. "I don't feel good," he said, and looked as if he was going to faint. In a few minutes he felt better, but in those few minutes the governor had changed his mind.

"I am taking no action, now or ever, on this application for a pardon for Billy the Kid because I do not believe this man is Billy the Kid."

The newspaper men went off to tell the world about it. "The bubble burst today for the buckskin-clad vain little man who claims he is 91 years old and is the one and only, the true Billy the Kid." That was the sort of comment made by all the reporters present.

Morrison took his client back to El Paso, expecting to renew his application when the next governor took office.

Brushy Bill was bitterly disappointed. He did not think he had been given a square deal. He felt worse because he had left for Santa Fe without telling his wife who he claimed to be and he was afraid she would leave him now that the cat was out of the bag. There was only one bright spot in the whole gloomy business- the fact that he would not have to go back to jail and was not going to be hanged. Otherwise it had been a bad show for him.

He returned to his little house in Hico, Texas, and went to bed for a while. In a few days he was up and around again, but the strain had been too much for him. About one o'clock on December 27 he went out to mail a package for his wife. Just as he was passing the office of the Hico News-Review, his heart stopped ticking and he died in the street with one arm across the bumper of a car parked at the curb.

That might have closed the chapter. For most people it did. But Brushy Bill was not giving up, even on the wrong side of the grave. He had made some attempts at writing his autobiography and had spent some time with Morrison correcting this narrative just before his death. Morrison had got some more of his recollections on a tape recorder and had taken notes on their innumerable conversations, especially the ones they had while traveling through New Mexico together. In his files were certified copies of legal papers, affidavits from old men and women, letters, and records of interviews with people who knew something about Brushy Bill. He was convinced that Roberts was really what he claimed to be and made up his mind that his man should have a hearing even if it had to be posthumous.

He showed his material to C.L. Sonnichsen, of the staff of Texas Western College, at El Paso, a transplanted Northerner who had made a hobby of Southwestern history and folklore. Sonnichsen had met Roberts for a few minutes once, before the fiasco in Santa Fe, and was not too much impressed by Brushy Bill's buckskin, boots, and badges until he reflected that a little exhibitionism was probably a normal part of the character of any frontier outlaw, including Billy the Kid.

He, naturally, was bothered by the fact that this sort of thing had happened so many times before. Old desperadoes never die; they do not even fade away. They arise from their ashes, full of strength and stories. Every year some graybeard comes forward claiming to be this or that notorious character of the past- and the great killers have provoked impersonation even before they were dead. John Wilkes Booth died in Texas long after he should have been moldering in his grave. Jesse James passed on at one hundred seven, not long after the demise of his friend Brushy Bill Roberts, and other men have appeared who called themselves by the name of the fabulous Jesse. Even such an innocuous but notorious figure as Oscar Wilde was said to have survived his funeral. Billy the Kid, himself, has been reported ever since 1881 as living in Mexico, in California, in Arizona, in New Mexico, in Texas, and in South America. Old men seem to fall naturally into these delusions. It is said that in recent years the caretaker at Roy Bean's old saloon in Langtry, Texas, grew a beard and began passing himself off as the original Law West of the Pecos.

This story could hardly be anything but a hoax, like all the rest of them-not worth paying any attention to. And yet, Sonnichsen thought, in this age of scientific attitudes, could one afford to be positive? Inductive reasoning establishes only a strong probability. Nine hundred and ninety-nine hoaxes do not prove that the thousandth case will be a hoax too. There are always exceptions to confound the skeptic and make him skeptical of his skepticism.

And there were things in Brushy Bill's story that made one wonder. How did he know that negro soldiers from Fort Stanton took position son the hillside and joined in the firing that day when the Murphy men burned McSween's house? Not many people know about that. How could he be sure of the layout of the second story of the Lincoln courthouse and jail when the experts argue about it? Billy was not the type to read up on these matters and remember every little detail.

And what about the killing of Jim Carlyle the day the posse cornered Billy the Kid at the Greathouse ranch? The stories say that Billy shot him when he dived through a window. Brushy Bill maintained that Carlyle was shot by the possemen, who thought it was the Kid crashing headfirst into the open. The Kid wrote a letter to Governor Wallace afterward- a letter that historians know about but ordinary readers to not- telling it exactly that way.

If Brushy Bill was not Billy the Kid, he must have been at the Kid's elbow when some of these things happened. His account would, at least, shed valuable light on what actually took place.

And suppose the old man turned out to be an impostor- he would be interesting for that very reason, if for no other. Of the thousand and one fakes who have tried to edge into the limelight, here was the only one who could be investigated; the only one, as Morrison puts it, "who had the guts to go before the governor of his state and ask for a pardon." Here was a Western Lazarus, risen from the dead with a six-shooter in each hand, who was willing to tell of his experiences behind the veil. Such a phenomenon had never been heard of before.

And there was one final thought. How strange it would be if the most famous American of all time should really survive into the Atomic Age; how ironic if, after almost seventy years of lying and running and hiding, he decided, with tears and tremors, to come out of the shadows- and nobody would believe him.

There would be a real story. If it were not true, it ought to be, and somebody should look into it.

Oscar Garrett, son of the immortal Pat, argued that to believe Brushy Bill is to question the veracity not merely of his father, but of "a whole generation"; for if Billy was not killed, practically everybody in southern New Mexico must have heard something about it and must have been accessory to a lie by keeping silent.

It may be so. But before we talk about that let's let Brushy Bill tell his own story.

CHAPTER ONE

BRUSHY BILL'S STORY

MY GRANDFATHER, Ben Roberts, settled in Nacogdoches, Texas, in 1835. In 1836 he helped Sam Houston free Texas from Mexico. My father was born eight miles from Lexington, Kentucky, March 8, 1832. He fought in the Civil War in the Southern Army, under Ross, until 1863. Then he joined Quantrill. After the war he went west as a cowboy.

"My mother's maiden name as Mary Adeline Dunn. Her native state was Kentucky. Sometime in the late fifties my father moved to Buffalo Gap, Taylor County, Texas. I was born at the Buffalo Gap on December 31, 1859, the last hour of the last day of the year."

Thus begins Brushy Bill Roberts' account of his own life, as set down in a series of paper-covered notebooks and corrected not long before his death.

Historians have accepted without much question the statement that Billy the Kid was born in New York City on November 23, 1859, to William H. and Kathleen Bonney, and that the birth announcement appeared in the New York Times on November 25. Morrison asked the Times for a photo static copy of the announcement and was told that no information about births appeared in that issue.

Morrison quizzed the old man about this story and was told that nobody would ever find a record of his being born in New York- that he never saw New York until he was a man. Morrison's notes then record the following conversation: "Do you know why they think Billy the Kid was born in New York?"

"Yes, because I first told them that in that country up there when I went up there in New Mexico. That's the reason they think it, yes."

"You told them that you were born in New York?"

"Yes, and that I came with Mrs. Antrim."

"You told the Coe boys that you were born in New York?"

"Yes, and I told them Mrs. Antrim was my mother, and that I wanted to go back home to see my mother."

"Well, what did they say?"

"I guess they believed it, but they should have known that Mrs. Antrim died in '74 before I went to that country. My mother died when I was about three years old, but I did not tell them."

"Do you know if other people in the country told stores [lies] about their family and whereabouts?"

"Why yes. I wasn't the only one who ran away from home and landed in that country. I wasn't the only bad man, either. Lots of fugitives went there to live under different names. Just like the James boys and Belle Starr. They came to Lincoln at times, but they did not tell who they were and why they were there. You know as well as I do that they have no proof on record that Billy the Kid was born in New York. Neither do they have any proof that Billy the Kid is dead.

FRONTIER MOTHER
Mary Adeline Dunn, wife of J.H. Roberts and mother of William H. Roberts a.k.a. Billy the Kid

They will never find any record that he was born in New York. In those days people did not care where you come from. Not many of them bothered to ask. Sometimes when they talked too much they didn't live very long. No, they didn't live very long. Garrett didn't bother to tell them everything he done before he came to that country either. He was just like the rest of us. He wasn't no angel either."

His real name, the old man said, was William Henry Roberts. At the age of three he changed it for what seemed adequate reason.

J.H. Roberts, his father, was not a suitable person to control the destiny of any child, least of all his own. "Wild Henry" was a rough and violent follow, and his war experiences, particularly his service with Quantrill, were not of the sort to civilize and refine him. This fact was plainly, and probably painfully, apparent to his relatives. Consequently, when Mrs. Roberts died in 1862 while her husband was gone to the wars, her kinfolks came to the baby's rescue. Mrs. Roberts' half-sister, Mrs. Kathrine Ann (Kathleen) Bonney, came down from the Indian Territory and took him away with her, being careful to avoid leaving her address lest the father should follow and claim his child.

They went first to Trinidad, Colorado, then to Santa Fe, and finally to Silver City, New Mexico. Young Billy Roberts lived with Mrs. Bonney (later Mrs. Antrim) and her mother until he was twelve years old, and passed as her son.

Apparently Mrs. Bonney covered her tracks well, for when the war was over and Wild Henry Roberts came back to Buffalo Gap, he was unable to learn where his son had been taken. Soon he was married again- this time to Elizabeth Ferguson, of Tennessee. She became the mother of James Roberts, who was some six years younger than his half-brother Billy. In later years Billy consistently called his father's second wife "Mother," carefully omitting all reference to the things that happened to him before he was twelve years old.

Morrison was unable to find any verification for the story that Billy left Silver City at the age of twelve after committing his first murder. He left, according to Roberts' story, in 1872, at that age, but it was to go back to Texas to see his people. He first stopped at Buffalo Gap, only to find that his father and step mother had moved. He located them at Carlton, Texas, and lived with them for about two years, which was as long as he could stand it. During this period he was known as "Kid Roberts," since he was small for his age.

The only good thing that could be said for old man Roberts was that he made his son proficient in roping, riding, and shooting.

"From the time I was big enough to ride, I've been in the saddle," he wrote in his old age, "beginning by riding behind my father on the old Chidam [Chisholm] trail on cattle drives, seeing thousands of head in a single drive....I was a pretty good rider for a kid, riding most of the yearlings that they would run up. From that I began riding the two-year-old colts that they older boys would run up from the range. That was great sport to my boy friends. An old man stepped up to my dad one day and said, "That boy of yours is going to get some of these boys killed." He was a Baptist preacher from Arkansas. My father told him if he didn't want his boys around where his boys were learning to ride, that he could keep them at home. "My boy is learning to be a bronc buster, and I believe he will learn if he don't get his neck broken.'"

KATHRINE ANN McCARTY
Brushy Bill said this woman was Billy the Kid's aunt

"My father raised a goodly bunch of horses. I would step out in the herd and get one and break it by him helping me. By the time I was fourteen I would bar no common horse. I picked a four-year-old black out of the bunch and broke him. He could pace or singlefoot as fast as a common horse could run. Coming in one Sunday evening, he said, "You will have to let the doctor have that horse.' I told him that I had already broken fourteen horses and would have to go back to the heard to get another. "If that is the way you feel about it, I can break horses for the other man as well as for you, and get paid for it." He drew a whip from his cow horse and like to have beaten me to death. It taken me about a month to get well. My mother doctored me up, but I didn't go back to the herd to get another horse."

"I left home as soon as I was well enough to travel, which was in May of 1874. From there I went to the Indian Territory by the way of the old Chittem Trail with a herd of cattle. "

"As my father had warned me that he would have the rangers to bring me back home, I took precautions to climb from my horse and get into the chuck wagon and cover up lest he find me as we passed through the towns, which was very few and far between."

"I quit this herd at Briartown. As I was prodding along the trail, a big dark-featured man on a bay horse came dashing up."

"Where you going, Son?"

"I could see no use in lying to him so I told him very bluntly, 'I'm running away from home.' And I told him why. He said, 'Climb up, Son'; you may have a place to stay with me.' So I figured that would be jail."

"We rode up to a place where I was sure he lived. He told me to go into the corral and throw a saddle on one of the horses there and bring it out. He called his cow dog and rode down across the prairie and drove up four good milk cows. Then he told me, 'Put the horses away and I'll tell you what will be done with you in the morning.'"

"So you may be sure I didn't rest good that night, as I figured I was jail bound next day."

"But early next morning, very much to my surprise, I found I had fell into the hands of Belle Reed, later known as Belle Starr, the great outlaw. She told me very plainly was I was to do. I was to go up on a mountain which overlooked the surrounding country, with a pair of field glasses, and be a sentry or guard for her. My instructions were if I seen one man or rider approaching, blow one blast upon a bugle. Or if two men were approaching, blow two blasts, and so forth. And she, Belle, would do the rest."

BELLE STARR

"My job was a general chore boy around the place. They would go away lots of times leaving no one there but Aunt Ann, the negro cook, and me. I would take a pack horse and go to town for provisions and ammunition for them. She would go with me to the Canadian River and see me across and meet me there coming back.

During the time I was there I met all the outlaws in the territory. It seemed to be a holdout for outlaws there. I got acquainted with the James boys and the Younger boys, Joe Shaw's bunch, Rube Burrow and Jim Burrow and their bunch. I have seen them bring in sacks of money and throw it on the bed and Belle would count it out and say, 'This is your part and this is my part." Two men would be sitting there holding six shooters."

"At one time an outlaw ordered me to saddle his horse, talking pretty rough to me, and Belle overheard him. She told him that I was her kid and she would protect me. She told him to saddle his own horse and the quickest way to get away was too slow, for she was marking him off her list. She said, 'Blackie, you keep away from that boy or I'll blow your brains out.'"

"In my practice Belle discovered I was a good shot with a rifle or six-gun and offered me a job as her right-hand man. The offer I at once refused, as I told her I did not like the outlaw trail. She saw that she could not make an outlaw of me and told me when I got ready to go I could go."

"At the end of three months she gave me nice clothes and fifty dollars in money, saying "Texas Kid, any time you want to come back, you have a home with me.' She carried me within about a mile of town and set me down."

"After leaving her, I went to my aunt's home in Silver City for a few months. When my aunt died, I went back to the Indian Territory and fell in with a bunch of cattle rustlers and I was just a lackey boy for them. I had to black their boots, clean up their saddles, and anything they said to do. They beat me, they banged me, they swore they would hang me if I didn't do it. One of the rustlers took a shine to me and gave me a small gun to protect myself from the other rustlers."

"They were fixing to beat up on me one day when I took a shot at a big rowdy, grazing his temple. My friend who had given me the gun stepped up and said, "Here, here, you have beat that boy enough. Try me for a change." At which he fell in and whipped four of them."

"The boss also liked me. He told me, 'Son if you can ride that buckskin hoss in there in the corral, I'll give him to you. Also the pick of them saddles in the shed. But mind you, Son, that hoss is a killer." I rode him after a nasty fight. He sunned his sides and his belly too. I tell you that hoss could buck."

"I left the ranch next morning for Dodge City, and at the end of five days, I reached that place. The wagon yard is the place I stopped to leave my horse and hunt something to eat. There was four men sitting by a camp fire eating supper, and they invited me to eat with them. I was thankful for the meal. One of the men said, 'Son, you have a nice hoss and saddle there.' I told them, 'Yes, and a high bucker, too.'"

"Next morning when I brought him out for a rub down, he began to buck at the end of my lariat. At which one of the men said, 'Son you cannot ride that hoss. There's not one in twenty that can.' I told them, 'I rode him here. I'll ride him away.'"

"'Well, Son, if you ride that hoss you need not look further for a job. You already have one with me." At which he gave me ten dollars saying, 'Son, make yourself to home. We'll leave here in about four days. We're starting on a long trip to the Black Hills of South Dakota.'"

"Someone who was acquainted with my father notified him that I was seen in Dodge City, Kansas. He at once wired to the officials to catch and hold me two months at which time he would come after me. But the city marshal only had a brief description of me. So he jailed the wrong lad. It was a lucky break for me as it gave me two months start on my dad. But never again could he get a trace of me, for I was on my way north- four of us and two pack horses."

The rest of Roberts' account of these early days is hard to follow. He fell into the company of a man he calls Mountain Bill, who decided to make a career of betting on Billy's skill as a rider. According to one of Billy's notebooks, they covered practically the entire West, Billy riding the worst horses the ranchers and show people could dig up for him, while Mountain Bill placed bets which netted him plenty. They were in Arizona and Montana and Oregon and Wyoming and Nebraska. No horse was too much for the Texas Kid, and he attributed his success to the fact that Mountain Bill had placed him with a band of Cheyenne and Arapaho Indians for training. "I trained with the Indians four months and came out an expert rider. They taught me to ride with a one-hold surcingle or a two-hold surcingle. Also, they taught me to ride with a mane hold." He was not at his best riding in a corral, but preferred to stage his contests "on the bald prairie. I learned to ride a lick saddle with one girt, without a choke rope. Neither did I use hobbled stirrups. I used loose-rowel O.K. spurs. I was supposed to ride anything that wore hair and contest it according to Cheyenne rules after the Indians turned me loose."

Apparently the boy started his career as a bronco buster at a place called the Daugherty ranch, in the Oklahoma Indian Territory. He concluded this chapter of his life by taking a trip to Arizona with Mountain Bill.

"Bill and I went to Arizona to visit with Bill's sister and brother-in-law. This was about the first of April, 1877. We worked a few months on the Gila ranch. I think that was the name. I left Mountain Bill here and went down to Mesilla, New Mexico, where I ran into Jesse Evans and the boys I had known before. I met Jesse in Silver City about 1870 or 1871 and went with him down into Old Mexico when I left Silver City. I knew Mel Segura right after I knew Evans. Jesse and me stayed at the ranch of Segura's uncle in Chihuahua State, Mexico."

"When I broke Segura from jail at San Elizario, we rode to his uncle's ranch in Chihuahua, where we hid for a few days. I don't remember how long. We stayed there lots of times. Segura went down into Mexico and I rode back to Messila, that summer of '77. Met Jimmy McDaniel, Billy Morton, Frank Baker, and Tom O'Keefe there."

CHAPTER TWO

THE FEUD BEGINS

"IN THE summer of '77 Tom O'Keefe and I left Mesilla for the Loving's Bend near Phoenix, New Mexico. We had a run-in with some Indians in the Guadalupe mountains and I got lost. Lost my horse in the mountains during the fight. I struggled through the mountains and wound up at the Jones place at Seven Rivers. My feet were all cut up. I had walked several days through mountain brush."

"Jim and John Jones were working for Chisum, so I went to work with them- I think up at Bosque Grande. Fran McNab was foreman. Later Chisum moved to South Spring, I think. Tom Storey, Miles Fisher, Walker, Goss, Black, and Ketchum worked there too, I think."

"Sally Chisum was already there when I went to work for Chisum. Sally was not Old John's daughter. She was his niece. Her daddy was all right then, though."

"I made a cattle drive to Dodge City that fall with Chisum's outfit. We went up the Loving Trail, I think. Or the Goodnight Trail; I don't remember now. Maybe both of them run cattle on that trail. That was before my time. It was a good wide trail that connected with the other trails further up."

"This was the time we had the tintype picture made at the end of the cattle trail in Dodge City."

AT THE END OF THE CATTLE TRAIL

Copy of the tintype Brushy referenced that was made in Dodge City in the fall of 1877. Left to right: Jim Jones, Bob Speaks (trail boss), John Jones, and Billy the Kid- the latter identified by Bill and Sam Jones, brothers of Jim and John Jones

"I bought my first horse in that country from Chisum when I went to work with the Jones boys. He had that little roan that was wild and could run, so I bought him and paid for him out of my pay from Chisum."

"I left Chisum and worked for Maxwell a short time at Bosque Redondo. Then I went over to Frank Coe's place on the Ruidoso. While there I run into Jesse Evans and Baker again. They took me to Murphy's cow camp in the Seven Rivers country. Evans and his gang stole cattle from Chisum, and some horses too. They still had some of the horses when I went to work with them at Murphy's Seven Rivers camp that winter. They had stolen this roan, too, but he got back to the ranch."

"Later on we got into an argument about my share of the bunch of cattle we cut out, and one of the horses I was supposed to get, and they welshed on the deal. Baker accused me of stealing the little roan that I rode up there on when I went to work with them. I told him I bought the horse from Chisum with my own money, and I aimed to keep him too, I did. I had both six-shooters on him when I said it, but Jesse knocked the right one down. I swung the other over with my left hand and held it right in his ribs while I told him. He told the boys to keep still or suffer the consequences, and begged me to leave peacefully."

"You know Jesse and I were nearly like brothers. We had roamed New Mexico, Arizona, Texas, and Old Mexico together. Jesse and I argued, and I nearly killed him one day in Lincoln, but I always felt close to him. I tried to spring him from jail in Stockton one time after they killed Chapman."

"I almost killed Baker and Morton that time. Guess I should have done it, but I didn't."

"Well, after Jesse told them to keep still, I jumped on my little roan pony and rode back toward Tunstall's ranch on the Feliz. I was on my way to Coe's place. I stopped at Tunstall's to get something to eat. We always rode up to ranch houses when we got hungry. I knew some of the boys there. Dick Brewer was foreman. Bowdre had left Chisum and went to Tunstall's. John Middleton, Doc Skurlock, Bob Widenmann, and lots of others were there too. Dick Brewer, the foreman, was a friend of Coe, and I told him I was headed back there, as I head had trouble with Murphy's men. After eating, that day, Tunstall said that I might as well stay there with the boys, so he hired me to ride for him. That's the way I met Tunstall."

JOHN TUNSTALL

"John Middleton was lots older than the rest of us. He was as mean as hell, a heavy drinker. Tom O'Folliard was about the age of Jesse Evans and me. Tom was a big fellow. Jesse and me were small.

Tom was good, but liked to drink some. Charlie Bowdre was older than us. He was a good man- could shoot quick. Rudabaugh was the toughest I ever knew. He was older and rougher and had been through lots of trouble. I saw him in Sonora after that shooting at Maxwell's when they thought they had killed me. He was calm; not easily excited. Tom Pickett and Wilson were not bad men. I don't remember of seeing them in that war up there. Skurlock wasn't a bad man. He was in the war, though. Hank Brown was from a good family, but he was mean. So was Fred Wayte. They left me on a cattle drive just before Skurlock or just after him. I don't remember now."

"Selman fought on our side in that cattle business in '78. I knew him in '77. He was always in trouble and my men helped him, too. He was a good shot and had lots of nerve, too, he did. I don't think he worked for Chisum on that ranch, but I don't know. He was up there with the rest of us."

"Tunstall had a store in Lincoln in opposition to Murphy and Dolan. McSween became a partner with Tunstall. Then Old John Chisum joined them. Murphy men had been rounding up Old John's cattle and selling them to the army at Fort Stanton. Then Chisum would pay us boys a dollar a head to get his cattle back. That is how the cattle war got started, if you want to know it. Tunstall got mixed up in it through McSween and Murphy's troubles. McSween had worked for Murphy as his lawyer. Later McSween joined forces with Chisum and the trouble got worse."

"The Murphy bunch had come to Lincoln before McSween and Tunstall got there. Murphy and Dolan had been filling government contracts for beef and provisions. McSween was hired by Murphy to prosecute the Chisum cowboys for cattle rustling. McSween found out that Chisum was only taking his own cattle from the Murphy boys, so he quit Murphy and started up with Tunstall, who had come in from England to settle in this country. He raised blooded horses and ranched cattle on the Feliz."

"From this time on there were two factions fighting to get the business. Each accused the other of cattle stealing. I guess both of them were right about it."

ALEXANDER MCSWEEN

"The Murphy bunch had the backing of the Santa Fe Ring, which included Tom Catron, U.S. District Attorney, and his brother-in-law. Of course they were not out in the open with it, but during the cattle war Old Tom took over the Murphy-Dolan property. All the politicians belonged to the Santa Fe Ring, even judges and attorneys."

"Brady, the sheriff, wasn't any better than anyone else up there.

He was a Catron man and he did just as they told him. He had threatened to kill Tunstall several times. That attorney that prosecuted me in Lincoln County that time and the judge too were Catron men. How could a person get justice among them? The law wasn't no good."

"Later on the governor was put out of office by the President of the United States."

"Tunstall and McSween were ranching together on the Feliz ranch of Tunstall's. McSween was taking care of the estate of Old Man Fritz. He collected on an insurance policy and Murphy claimed that Fritz, his former partner at Stanton, owed the money to him. They had a lot of trouble about McSween's law fee.

Finally, Murphy got a judgment or attachment against McSween and started to pick up partnership property of Tunstall's. We turned the cattle over to the law. Tunstall had a herd of fine horses of his own. He decided that we would drive the horses over to Lincoln and surrender them until the case was cleared up.

THE WEST END OF LINCOLN
Showing the rear of the Murphy Building, where Billy the Kid was confined

"On the eighteenth of February Tunstall picked Dick Brewer, me, Widenmann, and I believe that John Middleton went along with us with the horses on the drive to town. While we were on the way to Lincoln, a sheriff's posse, headed by Billy Morton, rode into the ranch. They found that we were gone to Lincoln so they started after us. Some of their boys took the cattle to Seven Rivers while the rest of them came after us. We had crossed the country and was well up in the mountains when we heard them coming.

We tried to get Tunstall to ride for it as we were outnumbered. He didn't want to leave his herd. He said that they wouldn't do anything, but we decided to run for it. We stood off and watched them approach the herd. They killed Tunstall in cold blood and went on into Lincoln. Afterward we rode in town and the boys went out and got Tunstall's body. None of the Murphy boys were present at the funeral of Tunstall when we buried his body behind the Tunstall store. And it was good for them that they stayed away. Tunstall was a good man. He had been good to me and treated me like a gentleman. I lost the best friend I ever had when they killed him. I swore that day that I would make them pay with their lives for this dirty deed.

"Judge Wilson, a friend of ours, swore in Dick Brewer as constable and gave him a warrant for the arrest of the murderers of Tunstall. Dick took me, Henry Brown, Fred Wayte, Charlie Bowdre, Frank McNab, and a few others to go after them. The hunt began for the murderers, who had left Lincoln for their hideout in the Seven Rivers country."

"We rode up on some of them and the fight began. Some of them got away, but we captured Billy Morton, the leader of the mob, and Baker.

Both of them had been good pals of mine until I left them at Murphy's cow camp a few months before. I should have killed them the day I left there."

"We put them on horses and started for the Chisum ranch, where we stayed overnight. The next morning we stopped at Roswell on our way to Lincoln. We knew that Murphy's boys would be waiting for us on the road to Lincoln, so we went the north road over the mountains. We stopped at Agua Negra in the Capitans where an argument started between one of our posse and Frank McNab. McNab had to kill one of our men during the argument. Then Morton and Baker started to run for it. I didn't want to take any chance of losing them, so I had to shoot them. We went on into Lincoln."

Brushy Bill's memories were apt to hit high spots. He returned again and again to the climactic episodes, particularly the ones in which he came near to losing his life, or in which he felt his part had been misrepresented. He was pretty clear about the next big event in the war- the killing of Sheriff William Brady- and he had reason to be, for that was the killing that brought Billy the Kid a death sentence. This is the way the story came out.

"Sheriff Brady was gunning for me with warrants for cattle stealing. He had caught us at Seven Rivers a short time before and arrested us. He took my six-shooter, a .44 single action with pearl handles that I paid twenty-five dollars for in San Antone. I thought lots of that pearl-handle .44. We got out on bond, but he said he didn't have that one six-shooter. He gave me a .44 with wooden handles. He still had the warrants and I knew he was still looking for me. He was a Murphy man and had some tough boys on his list of deputies. I didn't aim to be arrested anymore, I didn't."

"In the forenoon of April 1, Brady, his deputy, Hindman, and County Clerk Billy Matthews- I believe there was someone else, too- were coming down the street from Murphy's store to the old courthouse when we spied them. Henry Brown, John Middleton, and Fred Wayte were with me behind the adobe wall alongside of Tunstall's store. Matthews and I had a run-in a few days before, but my bullet missed him. As they passed along the wall, I leveled down on Matthews, but missed him. The other boys were firing at the same time. Brady fell dead on the spot. Hindman died soon after, but Matthews got away and ran behind an adobe wall down the street. Fred and I jumped over the wall and ran into the street where Brady was lying. I pulled my pearl-handled .44 off his body in time to catch a bullet from Matthews' rifle behind the adobe. It tore the flesh above my right hip and clipped Wayne through the leg. We got back over the wall, then rode out of Lincoln. I wasn't hurt much- never stopped riding- but Wayte was laid up for a few days. They were armed with rifles and six-shooters. They would have killed us if they had gotten the chance."

"Old Dad Peppin testified at my trial in Mesilla that I killed Brady. How did he know who killed anybody? He was the other fellow running down the street with Hindman and Matthews that day when Brady was killed. I was trying to get Matthews first. Nobody knows who killed Brady and Hindman. There was four against four. Nobody tried to find out who killed them, either."

Three days after Brady's death, on April 4, came the fight at Blazer's

Mill, in which Buckshot Roberts, a cranky but courageous old man, gave Billy the Kid and his gang more trouble than they could handle. Brushy Bill knew all about that battle too.

"I'll never forget that fight at Blazer's. Now you take that Buckshot. He was worse than any of them. He was out to get our scalps for the lousy money on our heads. He didn't fight in that cattle war. He was an outlaw before he went to that country, he was. He was a snake too, he was. But he got what was coming to him that day at Blazer's place."

"Buckshot was run out of Texas by the Rangers. He landed in Lincoln County. He came over to San Patricio, where I had a house, with Murphy's gang one time to raid us out. Then a few days before he come up to Blazer's, he stopped at my place in San Patricio and started an argument with Bowdre. I ran him off. Then he came back later as Charlie and I was leaving that night. He shot at us but we rode out of it. That's the reason I was trying so hard to kill him at Blazer's."

"We had warrants for his arrest. Dick was a deputy and we were with him. He got Brewer, though. Almost got me. But Bowdre got him."

CHAPTER THREE

BLOOD IN THE STREETS

THE THREE-DAY battle in Lincoln, July, 17, 18, and 19, 1878, was the end of the struggle for the McSween faction. It was a bloody business, and Brushy Bill Roberts described it as if every detail had been burned into his memory with a branding iron.

"John Copeland was appointed sheriff of Lincoln County to succeed Brady. He served until he was removed by the governor. Then Dad Peppin was appointed sheriff."

"Before he was appointed, Old Peppin worked for Coughlan, who was buying our cattle. We would take a herd of horses up to Tascosa to sell, and we drove cattle back for Coghlan at Three Rivers. Peppin skinned stolen cattle too, he did. That was rough country then. It was dog eat dog, that's all."

"Jimmy Dolan run the Murphy store in Lincoln in the Murphy building where I was in jail when I killed those two guards. They had large cattle interests and were selling to the army and the Indian agency. They would steal cattle from Chisum and we'd get them back for him."

"We were friends with Chisum until he lied to me over that cattle business. He promised to pay us boys a dollar a head to get his cattle back from Murphy. Then he didn't want to pay off. In that war he and

McSween promised to give us $500 apiece to fight for them. We'd have won that war too, if those nigger soldiers of Dudley's had been kept out. We had the Murphy gang whipped, we did."

"McSween had been hiding out at Chisum's ranch. They had threatened to kill him. We went over to the ranch to get him and bring him back to Lincoln. The sheriff's posse followed us and we had a fight right there at Chisum's. We whipped them and they left. We took McSween back with us, too, we did. As we rode into Lincoln, Peppin and his posse started to fighting us. The real battle broke out a little later when we took over Montana's house across the street from the tower where Peppin's posse was holed up. Some of our boys went into Tunstall's store and the rest of us went into McSween's house next door. They had filled Murphy's building with their men. They put men on the hillside just south of town until some of our men shot them loose."

"They started firing on us as we rode in that day, so we fought back at them. On the last day, Colonel Dudley rode into town with those nigger soldiers. He demanded that McSween stop the fighting. We told him, 'They started it- now go and stop them, will you? As long as they shoot at us, we intend to protect ourselves."

"He told McSween that he couldn't interfere, that the sheriff had the matter in hand. But he went and run some of our men out of town, he did. Why did he do that, if he couldn't interfere? Anyway we didn't surrender to the mob."

"Then they set fire to the building to smoke us out. We kept fighting all that day, though. We had them whipped until the army came into town. If we could have kept them niggers out there at Stanton, we would have whipped Peppin's posse. We didn't lose any men until that night. We had gotten a few of their men up there on the hillside."

"While the house was burning, Mrs. McSween entered Dudley's camp and begged him to stop the fighting. He said that he did not have the authority to interfere. But some of his nigger soldiers were up on the side of that hill firing at us with the Murphy men."

"By dark the house had burned, except the kitchen, which was nearly gone. About dusk in the evening, a little after dark, we decided to make a run for it. The women had already left the house. The building was caving in from the fire."

"There was a window in the east side of the kitchen. The door opened on the northeast corner into an area way between the house and an adobe wall. There was a board fence between the house and corral, running north and south, with a gate at the northeast corner of the yard. Tunstall's store building was east of the board fence on the other side of the corral where we kept the horses. Some of the murphy men were just across the river, which run past the north of the house. The gate in the board fence opened toward Tunstall's store."

"We opened the back door and looked out just as Bob Beckwith and some of them niggers started to come in."

"Harvey Morris, who was studying law with McSween, stepped out of the kitchen door first. I was right behind him, and Jose Chavez was behind me. Chavez was followed by McSween, Romero, and Samora. Morris was shot down in front of me. I ran through the gate with both .44's blazing, and Jose Chavez was right behind me. He and I ran toward

Tunstall's store, was fired at, and then turned toward the river. A bullet went through my hat as I come out the gate. Lost my hat and one six-shooter crossing the water. We ran down the other side of the river. There was brush and undergrowth all along there."

"We all left the house together, but McSween, Samora, and Romero were driven back by the bullets when they reached the gate. They turned and ran back to the small enclosure between the house and the adobe wall, where Bob Beckwith was standing as I came through the door. I think one of my bullets killed him there in that enclosure. They started for the gate the second time but were driven back to the small enclosure where all three were killed by John Jones, John Kinney, and those nigger soldiers of Dudley's. O'Folliard, Salazar, and the rest of our boys started through. All of them escaped except Salazar, who was cut down by the door. They thought he was dead. He crawled out that night after they left. He told me how McSween and the rest fell over there."

"I met Tom O'Folliard at Gallegos' house in San Patricio a few days afterward. Tom saw all of it. He was still in the burning house."

"We stayed at my place in San Patricio after that and tried to work on a ranch. We tried to settle down, but they wouldn't let me alone, they wouldn't. I wanted to make my home in this country, but they run me out. They made outlaws of us, that's all. We had to live some way. So we saw to it that we did make a living."

"I gathered up some of the boys and hung around Fort Sumner picking up cattle which belonged to anyone who could round them up. We were accused of stealing cattle. So was Murphy and

Chisum. The only difference between us and them is that they stole them wholesale and we just took them as we needed them. We thought we had a right to live, and we saw to it that we got along. Wouldn't you?"

"With Tunstall and McSween dead, Old John thought he could get out of paying us off, but he didn't, he didn't. We told him if he didn't pay us that we were going to run off enough of his cattle to pay what we thought he owed us. We cut cattle out of his herd and he didn't do anything about it. We got our share, and more too, maybe. But who knows?"

"I tried to get him to pay us. I told him the quickest way he could do it was too slow. I had my six-shooter in his ribs, and I don't know why I didn't put him in a six-foot grave. From then on Old John was our bitterest enemy."

"The country was full of bad men in those days. We were not by ourselves. The only difference was they had the law and the politicians on their side. The law was just as crooked as the rest of us."

"I didn't kill that Indian agent. I had nothing to do with it. I got blamed for it, of course. I got blamed for everything that no one else wanted. We were up there, but we did not go to steal horses like they say we did, No sir!"

Chapter Four

To Be Hanged by the Neck

BRUSHY BILL ROBERTS could not talk about the events which followed the burning of the McSween's house without betraying great excitement, and sometimes shedding tears. Well, why not? Every minute was bringing him closer to the noose.

"About this time," his story went on, "the President removed the governor from office in Santa Fe. He sent General Wallace to take over as governor of the territory. Mrs. McSween and John Chisum talked with the governor about conditions in the country. It looks like things would straighten out. The governor issued a Proclamation of Amnesty to most of the people who had fought in that war. It did not apply to me. I already had indictments against me for the murder of Brady and Hindman. But I didn't kill them, I didn't. I wasn't even shooting at them. How could I kill them?"

"Most of that fall and winter we stayed around Fort Sumner and Portales. In the winter of '79 we got together with Dolan and Evans and agreed to quit fighting each other."

"When we came out of the saloon that night in Lincoln we run into Chapman, the lawyer for Mrs. McSween. Campbell and Dolan killed him in cold blood. I was standing there with them and saw who killed him."

"I heard that Governor Wallace had offered a thousand dollars for me if I would come in and testify. I wrote and told him that I would come in if he would annul those indictments against me. He wrote back that he would meet me at Squire Wilson's house in Lincoln- that house out there by the tower."

"I tied my horse up while Tom watched and went up to the back door. The governor and Wilson were alone in the house. I went in and talked for several hours. I explained that Tom and I had seen them shoot Chapman in cold-blooded murder. He wanted us to testify before the grand jury and tell them what we knowed. Also he wanted me to testify against Colonel Dudley in his court martial trial at Stanton. I told him about things in general in this country and what started the trouble. I was not afraid to talk like the rest of them. I had the guts to help the governor out. No one else would say enough to help him."

GOVERNOR LEW WALLACE

"This happened to me one night in March. We didn't meet like they say we did in the daytime at Patron's. I had only this one meeting with Wallace until I submitted to arrest. The governor did come there after Tom and I were arrested. We were kept at Patron's that time, I think."

"He promised to pardon me if I would stand trial on my indictments in the district court in Lincoln, testify before the grand jury in the Chapman case, and testify against Dudley. I promised to do it and Tom and I left for San Patricio, where he lived with me."

"General Wallace sent Sheriff Kimbrel to San Patricio to pick us up. He let me pick the men to arrest me. Tom and I went to Lincoln with them and went to jail."

"When my case was called, Judge Leonard was not there. The court appointed Colonel Fountain to represent me. I plead not guilty to the indictments. Then we went before the grand jury that brought in the indictment against Dolan and his men for the murder of Chapman. I testified at the Dudley trail in Stanton. Then they wanted to take me to Mesilla for trail on my indictment."

"I had promised the governor that I would stand trial in Lincoln and not any place else, to which he agreed. It begun to look now like the governor could not do like he wanted. The judge was a Murphy sympathizer and a friend of Tom Catron at the head of the Santa Fe Ring. I saw that they did not intend to treat me right. I went to Kimbrel and told him to give me my scabbards and six-shooters. He said he could not blame me as it looked like I was being taken for a ride. I did ride, but not to Mesilla. Tom and I walked out of the jail.

We rode back to Fort Sumner and told them if they wanted us, to come and get us. But come a-shootin'. They never arrested anyone else for the Brady murder. They never tried to arrest anyone else. They didn't do like they promised me. They pinned the whole affair on me, because they wanted to get rid of Billy the Kid. But they didn't hang me, they didn't."

There was a good deal of skirmishing after Billy the Kid walked out of the jail at Lincoln. As he increased the tempo of his activities as a cattle and horse thief, the law speeded up its efforts to catch him. Brushy Bill did not have much to say about these minor run-ins, but he did have vivid recollections of the fight at the Greathouse ranch or road house in November, 1880- possibly because he thought Billy the Kid got an especially raw deal there.

GEORGE KIMBREL

"I don't know where Greathouse's ranch was. That has been a long time to recollect, that has. But while we were there, we were surrounded by a posse. Surrounded by a posse, we was. They sent in Carlyle to get us to surrender. He had no warrant. I just told him that it amounted to mob violence, and we didn't intend to be mobbed. Not just yet, anyhow. The posse had Greathouse with them. When they commenced shooting out there, Carlyle got scared and jumped through the window. As he went out through the window, they shot him down without warning. They thought it was me making an escape, but they got fooled that time. We were going to make Carlyle ride out with us after dark. They left, and we got out that night."

"The next day they came back and burned down the house, thinking that we were on the inside. They were like rats. They burned us out of McSween's house and they were trying the same thing again. But we beat them to it again, we did. We went to Las Vegas, where I read that Billy the Kid had killed Carlyle. I wrote to Governor Wallace and told him that I did not kill Carlyle. That his own men killed him. But I got blamed for that killing too. Garrett told me about it later on."

"Garrett had been a deputy under Sheriff Kimbrel. Kimbrel run for re-election. Old John Chisum, Lea, and several others put Garrett up against Kimbrel. They knew that Kimbrel was a friend of Governor Wallace and a friend of Billy the Kid. Garrett won the election."

"He had not been in the country long. He come here from Texas, where he killed a man, a partner, in a quarrel over dividing buffalo hides. We knew about it. We traveled through Texas too. Garrett had nothing when he landed in Fort Sumner. Me and my boys bought him the first pair of boots he over owned in this country. We paid for the celebration at his first wedding in Fort Sumner. He rode with us, gambled and danced, but now he turned coat."

"He went to work for Maxwell when he landed in Fort Sumner, but he didn't last long. He bought in with Beaver Smith, who had a saloon and lunch room in Fort Sumner. The people around there had no use for him. They were all our friends."

"With this killing of Carlyle tacked on me, Garrett had another excuse to go after me, which he did. We were riding to Fort Sumner one night in a snow storm that December about eight o'clock. Garrett and his posse took over Bowdre's home and were there waiting for us to come in. O'Folliard had been living with Bowdre and his wife there. As we rode in, I took another road, thinking they might be watching for us. Tom and the boys rode up to Bowdre's and they started shooting at my boys, hitting Tom. I heard the shooting and rode in, to find the boys leaving town."

"They carried Tom inside and let him die, begging for water to drink. His cousin, Kip McKinney, one of Garrett's posse, wouldn't give Tom a drink when he was dying. Tom was a better man than McKinney. Tom's uncle on the Texas Rangers did not let him down, but the brave McKinney did it, he did. I met Cook, Tom's uncle, in Roswell in the fall of '80. He wanted to talk to Tom, but I wouldn't let him. I told him Tom was my best pal and I needed him. I wouldn't let him go yet. Later on I wished I had.

HE NEVER GOT BACK TO TEXAS
Tom O'Folliard, Billy's right-hand man, killed by Garrett's posse before he could carry out his plan to leave New Mexico

After a couple of days riding in the snow, we landed at the old rock house at Stinking Springs. We brought a couple of our horses inside and tied the others outside from the gable of the roof. The next morning at sunup Charlie Bowdre went out to feed the horses. When he stepped through the door opening (there wasn't any door), Garrett and his posse fired from ambush without warning, wounding Charlie seriously. He wore a large hat like mine. They thought he was me. They didn't intend to give the Kid a chance. They knew when he went down, he would take some of them with him."

"Charlie walked back in, but when he went back after them, he fell dead. We stayed in there all day, planning to ride out after dark. As we were trying to lead the other horses inside, they shot a horse and he fell over in the doorway. I had intended to ride my mare out on her side, like the Cheyenne Indians taught me in my boyhood days, but my mare wouldn't jump over the dead horse in the doorway, so we gave up the idea. I would have ridden out a-shooting if that dead horse had not fell over in the opening. They promised to protect us if we would surrender. We threw out our six-shooters and filed out the door. They loaded us in a wagon with Bowdre's body and took us to Fort Sumner. The next day they buried Bowdre near O'Folliard, who they killed a few days before."

KILLED BY MISTAKE
Charles Bowdre, who fell before Garrett and his posse at the old rock house in
December, 1880- shown here with his weapons and his wife

"The next day Mrs. Maxwell sent her Indian servant over to ask Pat Garrett if he would let me visit with them before taking me to Santa Fe to jail. Dave Rudabaugh was chained to me when Jim East, a friend of mine from Tascosa, Texas, and another member of the posse took us over to Maxwell's house. The Indian was wearing a scarf that she had just made from angora goat hair. I traded her my tintype picture in my shirt pocket for this scarf. I wore the scarf around my head on the trip to Las Vegas, after we left Maxwell's house."

DAVE RUDABAUGH

"After we went in the house, Mrs. Maxwell asked them to cut me loose from Rudabaugh so I could go into another room with her daughter. They refused to do it. They suspected it was a trap to let me escape. I knew if they did let me in the other room, that they would go back to Garrett without me. I knew that I would find shooting irons in that room. And I knew that I would be able to use them. They knew that the handcuffs would not bother me. That's why they would not take off the leg irons. Anyway they would not cut me loose from Dave."

"We went back and started for Las Vegas, where we arrived a couple of days later. I almost got away from them at the jail in Las Vegas. The next day they put three of us on the train for Santa Fe, and it looked like trouble before we started out of there. I told Pat if he would give me a six-shooter that I would shoot it out with the mob and stay with him the rest of the trip."

"At Santa Fe we were put in jail. I wrote to Governor Wallace to come and talk to me, but he failed to do so. Sherman would not let my friends visit me in the jail, but he would let curiosity seekers in to look at me as if I was a dog. The governor had forgotten his promise to help me. They took me to Mesilla the last of March to stand trial on my indictments. We left Santa Fe on the train and wound up in Mesilla on the stage."

"In April I pleaded to the federal indictment and it was thrown out of court. Judge Leonard represented me on this indictment. He got it thrown out by the judge. Then I was put on trial for the murder of Sheriff Brady, a territorial charge."

"Again I was treated like a dog. They took me in court every morning chained and handcuffed. Olinger was there as a U.S. deputy marshal. He taunted and threatened me constantly. I tried for a six-shooter on one of the guards one day, but I couldn't quite reach it. I'd have killed Olinger first if I could have gotten it. They sat me up front near old Judge Bristol, who I had threatened to kill before. He was scared all the time I was in court in Lincoln and in Mesilla. He knew that he was looking for a six-foot grave if I got loose."

THE INFAMOUS TINTYPE
The tintype of Billy the Kid traded to Deluvina Maxwell by Billy the Kid. Historically, the only authenticated photo of "the Kid" to exist.

"Judge Fountain was appointed to represent me on the territorial charge. He done all he could for me. I had no money. Couldn't get any. They didn't sell my mare up at Scott Moore's in Las Vegas. He was a friend of mine, but now he said I owed him money for board."

"The trial was crooked. I asked for witnesses which they could not find. They didn't want to find them. Sheriff Garrett knew where they were. Hank Brown was in Tascosa when I was on trial. Garrett knew it, too, but he didn't do anything about it. I think they turned Billy Wilson loose at Mesilla. I don't think he was tried in court, but I don't remember."

"The trial lasted about a week. They jury found me guilty of the murder of Sheriff Brady, and Judge Bristol sentenced me, on April 13, to hang on May 13 in Lincoln County. My other indictment was throwed out of court the next day."

"On April 16 they loaded me on an old Army ambulance, handcuffed, shackled, and the leg shackles chained to the back seat, and we started for Staunton. John Kinney, who fought against me in the war, sat on the back seat beside me. Billy Matthews, who had shot me and Wayte when Brady was killed, sat across and facing Kinney. Deputy U.S. Marshal Bob Olinger, my bitterest enemy, sat beside Matthews and facing me, threatening to kill me all the time on that trip to Stanton. Dave Woods and a couple other guards rode horseback, one on each side, and the other rode behind the ambulance. They told me if anyone attacked that they would kill me first and then catch the other fellows. We left Mesilla a little before midnight so no one would know where we were. As we were sleeping one night, I almost got away from Matthews, who was guarding me at the time. It took about five days to make the trip to Fort Stanton, where Garrett picked me up and took me to the jail in Lincoln."

CHAPTER FIVE

JAILBREAK

WHAT HAPPENED in the Lincoln County jail in 1881 was still giving Brushy Bill Roberts the horrors sixty-nine years later. In August, 1950 he came back to Lincoln for the first time in many decades. He was riding with Morrison, who was on his way to Carrizozo to go through the records in the county courthouse. They stopped in front of the place where Billy the Kid passed the long days and nights waiting for his death sentence to be carried out. Roberts was very uneasy and cried intermittently. He refused to get out of the car and go inside. Morrison went in alone and had a chat with Mr. Wright, who was pinch hitting for Colonel Fulton, the custodian.

That night, after Morrison had gone through the records at Carrizozo, they talked far into the small hours about what had happened in the old days, but it was not till the next morning, when they were back-trailing toward Roswell, that things began to come alive for the old man. The country had changed so much in seventy years that he had trouble locating himself, but suddenly he pointed to the mountainside on the right. "Over there," he said, "was a rock ledge that we used to ride out on and fire down into the valley. A little farther down on the other side of the road, we ought to see a cave we used to use."

Sure enough, the cave came into view. "A man could get a horse in there," he remarked.

Back in Lincoln he still refused to visit the old courthouse. But just as they reached the outskirts of town, headed for Roswell, he changed his mind. "Let's go back to that place," he said. "I might go inside if there's nobody there."

He sat in the car while Morrison reconnoitered. Mr. Wright was still the only official present, so Bill got out and came in. Mr. Wright was very courteous and showed them some of his relics. They came to a pair of leg irons of the type Billy was wearing when he escaped. Bill thought Mr. Wright was passing them off as the genuine originals, took offense, and nearly let his tongue run away with him.

"Them are not the leg irons that Billy the Kid rode out of here with. I ought to know that Billy's leg irons were cut apart in the middle of the chain."

Then he bethought himself, turned red, counted the links in the chain to the number of fourteen, and agreed that the shackles were of the type that Billy wore.

When Mr. Wright's back was turned, he whispered to Morrison, "If you think its safe, I would like to go up there and show you where I was locked to the floor in that room on the corner." Morrison reassured him and they mounted the stairs to the second floor.

Upstairs, Bill seemed nervous and somehow lost, as if he were trying to find a familiar landmark in a wilderness. The stairs inside were about the way they had been, but he remarked that there was no outside stairway to the balcony in the old days. The upper floor was completely changed. He explained to Morrison how it had looked in 1881.

"The stairway began on the first floor on the west side, running east into the large hall which run north and south in the building. At the east end of this hall a door opened into Garrett's office. On the east side of Garrett's office a door opened into the room where I was confined in the northeast corner room. Across the hall from Garrett's office door was another door opening into the armory room."

He walked over to one of the eastern windows.

"I was sitting right here on a soap box that morning," he said, "when Olinger loaded his shotgun with buckshot, twelve in each barrel. He snarled at me as usual and said, 'Kid, do you see these buckshot I am loading into these two barrels, twelve in each barrel? Well, if you try to make a break, I'll put all twenty-four between your shoulder blades.'"

"I said, 'Bob, you might get them before I do and I smiled at him. Then he brought out a lariat rope and said, "This is good enough to hang you with." I told him a lariat rope was not fit to hang a man with."

"At noon time, as usual, Olinger went across the street with the other prisoners for lunch and left Bell there guarding me. Olinger and Bell were always on guard duty. Olinger always brought me lunch when he came back. Then Bell would go for lunch. During the week I was kept here, I was guarded constantly. They were afraid I would break jail or be rescued by my friends."

"It seemed that Bell lived in the neighborhood of White Oaks. He was a nice man. He treated me like an ordinary prisoner. But Olinger treated me like a dog."

"Olinger – wasn't nothing to him. A big bluff and a big coward. Killed all his men by shooting in the back or before they knew what was happening. He was a big fellow, too. Garrett didn't like him, either. I think the Beckwith family was related to Olinger's, but I'm not sure. Beckwiths were all right when they came to that country. Until Murphy turned them against Chisum, who helped them when they came to that country. Old John helped lots of them in that day."

"Olinger had worked for Chisum and was not liked by any of his boys. He had shot John Jones in the back in a camp on the Pecos. He murdered the Jones boy in cold blood. I promised the father that I would even the score with Olinger for this murder of his son. During my trial in Mesilla he kept taunting and teasing me. I was eager to kill him, but I did not want to kill Bell."

"The day before I got away, Sam Corbett and his wife came in to see me. Sam had hid a six-shooter in the latrine. So the next morning I planned to wait until Olinger took the rest of the prisoners to lunch and Bell would be alone with me, when I would ask him to take me to the latrine. I expected him to take me in there and I would come out a-shooting. But I didn't need Sam's six-shooter."

"Olinger is gone to lunch. Bell and I are alone in the building. I am sitting about here on a box, handcuffed, shackled, and chained to this floor with a lock. Bell is sitting over by that window and reading a paper. I asked Bell to unlock this chain and take me to the latrine downstairs. At first he objected; said he didn't know. Then he went into that room [Garrett's office] and got the key to unlock this chain. At this moment I slipped my right hand from the cuff and holding them in my left, I hit him in the back of the head. He tumbled over on the floor. When he come up, he was looking down the barrel of his own six-shooter."

"I told him that I would not hurt him if he would do as I said. I told him to walk through that office and unlock the armory door as I wanted to lock him in there until I could escape. Without saying a word, he walked through the office. When he stepped into the hall, he ran for the stairway. With the fourteen-inch chain between my leg irons, I could not run, so I jumped and slid across the floor to the left toward the stairs. When he reached the third or fourth step, my left hand was nearing the stairs. I pulled the trigger and the bullet struck the wall on that side. It must have ricocheted and struck him under the arm, coming out on the other side. Bell fell down the steps, dying as he fell."

"I turned and scuttled back to the office, where I picked up Olinger's shotgun where he stood it against the wall that morning. I went over to my window. When I looked out, I saw Olinger and another man coming over across the street toward the jail. Just as Olinger came across the street, he put his six-shooter into the scabbard. He probably thought that Bell had killed me in the jail. As he came near the corner of the building beneath my window, I levelled down on him, saying, "Look up, Bob. I want to shoot you in the face with your own buckshot. I don't want to shoot you in the back like you did other men, and the Jones boy." The buckshot struck him in the breast, killing him instantly. Then I fired the other twelve into him. I wanted him to get all of them like he had promised to give them to me. I wanted him to know that I was the man who was killing him."

"This was the happiest moment of my life. I promised to give him his own buckshot while he was loading the gun that morning. He shot the Jones boy in the back of the neck, killing him. He threatened to put the shot from both barrels in my back, and he would have done it if he would have had the chance. That was his way of killing other men, but he did not die that way."

"I went downstairs and out the side door at the bottom of the stairs, where Old Man Goss and someone else were standing near Bell's Body. I told Goss to cut this chain between my legs. He tried to cut it with a saw. I told him to get the axe and cut it "and be damn careful where you hit that chain." I held a .44 on him. He cut the chain as I stood over the rock. I took and tied each end of the chain to my belt so I could straddle a horse. Goss caught the horse behind the jail in the pasture. He and the Gallegos boy saddled the horse and took him to the front of the jail. I went back upstairs to this armory room and picked up a .44 Winchester belt loaded with cartridges and crossed it over my other shoulder, picking up a Winchester and two .44 single-action Colts with scabbards."

"As I walked out on the balcony upstairs here, everything was calm with no one trying to catch me. No one wanted to fight. I called out that if anyone was looking for a six-foot grave, that they should follow me."

"I went back downstairs and out to the front of the jail, where the horse was tied. I jumped for the saddle, but slid off the other side, hanging to the rope. The Gallegos kid went down the road and took a rope off a yoke of steers in the field and tied it to my saddle. I got on the horse and rode out of Lincoln to the west and up the canyon to the home of a friend, who cut the bolts in my leg irons. After they screwed the nuts on the bolts, they riveted over the ends of the bolts so I couldn't unscrew them with my hands."

All the while this recital was going on, the old man was in tears and greatly excited. It was as much as he could stand to be in that room. He took one last look around and headed for the stairs. Morrison loaded him into the car and they drove off.

They passed the building twice in later expeditions, but Brushy Bill would never go back inside. One time Colonel Fulton came out to shake hands and ask him in, but once was enough; he would not get out of that car.

After leaving the building, he had an idea that he would like to see if he could retrace his escape route up the canyon, but the country had changed so much since the last time he was there (in 1892, he said) that he couldn't see anything that looked familiar. Morrison turned around and took up the route to Roswell, Bill filing in with more reminiscences as they drove.

"I turned the horse back for Lincoln and walked over the mountain. My guns began to get heavy and I hung one of them in the fork of a tree. I was headed for the house of Higinio Salazar. We had been friends for a long time. I had stayed with him and his mother before. Neither of us were married. His brother might have been married. I don't remember. I knew if I could reach his house across the mountain, he would help me as much as he could."

"Higinio was the one who escaped from the burning McSween

building. He was seriously injured, but he recovered. I walked near the house and whistled several times before he came outside. He recognized me and we talked about my escape. He urged me to leave for Old Mexico. I argued that I would not leave the country until I killed Old John, Barney Mason, and Garrett. He went back in the house and brought a blanket for me. I slept in the underbrush, as I thought a posse would be looking for me and I did not expect to die alone."

"Next day he brought food to me. On the second day he borrowed a horse and I started for Fort Sumner across the plains. I told him about hanging my pistol in the tree and he tried to find it, but never could."

"While on my way the horse broke loose and left me on foot again. I walked into Anaya's sheep camp below Fort Sumner and stayed a few days. I traveled at night and slept in the daytime. I expected Garrett down at Fort Sumner hunting for me. After dark one evening I walked to the home of Charlie Bowdre's widow, where I spent the night, and the next day or so. From here I rode back to Garcia's. I rode around Fort Sumner with some ranchers and herders for about two and a half months before I had the fight with Garrett's posse that night in July. I would not leave until I had killed Chisum, Barney Mason, and Garrett."

"It was about the middle of May, 1881, when I rode out to Old John's ranch on South Spring. I met a Mexican cowboy. I pulled down on him, telling him to go in and bring Old John out so I could talk to him in my language. He told me that Old John was not in there. I promised him that I would kill him if I find out that he is lying to me. I stayed at a camp nearby for a few days watching and waiting until I found out the Mexican was telling the truth. I left there looking for Barney Mason. He started to ride up to the camp where I was staying. When I came out, he left and mighty quick, too, he did. I could have killed him if I had known it was him."

"I sent a note to Garrett that I was waiting for him, and that he had better come a-shooting, too. They had both been good friends of mine until Chisum and others had Garrett elected sheriff of Lincoln County. We rode and gambled together. Mason rustled cattle and horses with us after Garrett was elected. But when he started squealing to Garrett, we ran him off."

"I knew Celsa and Pat's wife, who were sisters to Saval Gutierrez, before Pat came to this country. Celsa was one of my sweethearts when I was in Fort Sumner. Her brother, Saval, lived in Fort Sumner. After I returned from hunting Old John, he went up to Canaditas and got Celsa for me. She wanted to go to Mexico with me, but I did not want to get married until Garrett was gone."

"While I was in Fort Sumner I stay at Gutierrez', Jesus Silva's, and Bowdre's. I also stayed at the Yerby ranch north of Fort Sumner quite a bit. We were good friends. I kept horses and mules there when Charley Bowdre worked for Yerby. He had a good-looking daughter, who was sort of a sweetheart of min. I don't remember her name. Fort Sumner had some good-looking girls in those days."

"Most of my time was spent at the Yerby ranch after I broke jail in Lincoln. There were several cow and sheep camps on the road from

Yerby's to Fort Sumner. I stopped off in most of them during the day time."

CHAPTER SIX

DEATH BY MOONLIGHT

"I RODE into Fort Sumner from Yerby's a few days before Garrett and his posse rode in. When they rode in that day, I had spent the day with Garrett's brother-in-law, Saval Gutierrez. Nearly all the people in this country were my friends and they helped me. None of them liked Garrett. Garrett and his posse came in that night while we were at a dance. Silva saw Garrett in Fort Sumner a little while before we rode in from the dance. He knew I was staying with Gutierrez, so he went over there to warn me to leave town. Gutierrez told him we were out to a dance."

"When my partner*, me, and the girls rode into town, we stopped at Jesus Silva's. Jesus told Celsa that Garrett was in town looking for the Kid. About midnight the girls left and I began asking him about Garrett. He got excited and told us to leave before Garrett found us there. I thought Garrett would go to Gutierrez', and I had better stay away that night. I told Silva that we was not going to leave until we had something to eat. He agreed to fix a meal for us."

*This was the man Brushy Bill called Billy Barlow, and here we strike the weakest link in his narrative. No references to such a man have, so far, turned up in the records, and Bill himself could not contribute much. He said he had worked on the Muleshoe ranch with Barlow, but was doubtful that this was the boy's actual name. He thought Barlow had come into the country that winter (1880) and had taken no part in the cattle war. Barlow was younger than Billy the Kid, but about the same size. He drank heavily—had been drinking at the dance the night of the supposed killing of Billy the Kid. Brushy Bill told Governor Mabry, during the interview in Santa Fe, that he and Barlow looked very much alike. He seemed to think that Barlow was connected with the Clements family, to which John Wesley Hardin also was related. Perhaps one of the many Clements descendants now living in Texas and New Mexico may know something about him.

"He was cooking the meal for us to eat when my buddy asked for fresh beef. Silva said if one of us would go over to Maxwell's and get beef, he would cook it for us. I sensed a trap, but my partner insisted that we go get the beef. He started out to Maxwell's after I refused to leave Silva's house. I thought that Garrett might still be in town, and I wanted to meet him in the daytime so I could beat him to it. In a short time we heard pistol shots. I ran through the gate into Maxwell's back yard in the bright moonlight and started shooting at the shadows along the house. One of their first shots had killed my partner on the back porch.* After entering the yard, their first shot struck me in the lower left jaw, taking out a tooth as it went through my mouth."

*The late Jack Fountain, son of Colonel Fountain (whose disappearance in the neighborhood of the White Sands is southern New Mexico's most famous murder mystery) gave C.L. Sonnichsen a new version of the shooting at Pete Maxwell's in an interview on April 15, 1944. "I rode with Pat Garrett for weeks at a time," he said, "and on one occasion he finally said, "Well, I'll tell you the whole story. After Billy got away after killing Olinger and Bell (and Olinger got what was coming to him), the county commissioners wished that job on me. I didn't want it, but that $10,000 looked good. I thought about what I knew of the Kid and his habits—heard there was to be a dance at Portales— went over. The Kid was just in off the range when we arrived and tied our horses. He went to the house of a woman across the street and said, "I'm hungry. Can you cook something for me?" She said, "Don Pedro has just killed. You go across and cut some meat and I'll fix you a good meal." He went across, suspecting nothing. The beef was hanging in a little outer room from the vigas. There was a candle and materials for making a light in a niche in the wall. He made a light and held it up while he cut. I was in Pete's room, talking. Billy heard something and asked Pete who was there. Pete said, "Nobody." I looked out at a perfect target—Billy lighting himself up with the candle. At first I was just going to wing him. Then I thought if he ever got to his gun it was him or me. My conscience bothers me about it now.""

This, of course, is only one of many variations on the theme of exactly how Pat got his man, but it is probably the only one which places the victim outside Maxwell's bedroom.

IT HAPPENED HERE
Pete Maxwell's House. His bedroom was at the front corner

"As I started over the back fence, another shot struck me in the back of my left shoulder. I had emptied one of my .44's when another shot struck me across the top of my head and about an inch and a half back of the forehead and about two inches in length. This shot knocked me out and I stumbled into the gallery of an adobe behind Maxwell's yard fence. A Mexican woman was living there and she pulled me in through the door."

"When I woke up, she was putting beef tallow on my head to stop the flow of blood. I told her to reload my .44's, which she did. "I started to go back out after them when Celsa came running in and said that they had killed Barlow and they were passing off his body as mine. She begged me to leave town. She said that they would not leave Maxwell's house for the night. They were afraid of being mobbed. "About three o' clock in the morning Celsa brought my horse up to the adobe. I pushed my .44's into the scabbards and rode out of town with Frank Lobato. We stayed at the sheep camp the next day. Then I moved to another camp south of Fort Sumner, where I stayed until my wounds healed enough to travel."

"Around the first of August I started for El Paso, where I had lots of friends. I crossed the Rio Grande north of town and went into Sonora, Mexico, where I was acquainted with the Yaqui Indians. I lived with them nearly two years."

BILLY THE KID SLEPT HERE

Brushy Bill said that Billy was staying in one of these old barrack rooms when Garrett tracked him down. Taken from the Parade Ground, looking east

---

CHAPTER SEVEN

FROM THEN UNTIL NOW

AFTER SO much gun smoke, blood, and passion, the later life of any man involved in the Lincoln County War would inevitably seem anticlimactic. And so it was with Brushy Bill Roberts. He had adventures enough, but nothing to compare with the high drama of the great cattle feud. If Brushy Bill was Billy the Kid, he gave up the role of Avenging Angel to become a broncho buster.

Just what he did after 1881, and when and where he did it, is not too easy to make out, in spite of the copious notes and bits of narrative he left behind. Bill was full of elaborations and evasions. Maybe he had reasons for leaving a crooked trail. Any any rate, here is the story he told, eliminating as many of the crooks and turns as possible.

"In the fall of '82 I left Mexico and went to Grand Saline, Texas. I was dressed like an Indian and I took a job driving a salt wagon from there to Carlton, where my folks had lived. I hoped to be able to find them there. I made two trips hauling salt, but never found my folks."

"I went back to Sonora, Mexico, where I stayed until the winter of '83. At this time I returned to Texas as the Texas Kid. I worked a short time at the Powers Cattle Company. From there I went up to Decatur, Texas, where I struck up again with Indian Jim. I had worked with Jim in No Man's Land in '75, and again in Arizona on the Gila ranch in the spring of '77."

"While on a cattle drive in Kansas City, I was arrested and held by the law as being Billy the Kid. The boys got me off, though."

"Then Indian Jim and I went to work for Tom Waggoner, at Decatur, breaking horses. Late in the winter we left for the Black Hills of Dakota. We joined the scouts, guarding the stage lines on the Idaho trail. We stayed with the scouts for about three or four years. During this time I earned the name of Brushy Bill from riding in the brushy hills of the Dakotas."

"Oftentimes we stopped in Cold Creek, Idaho, where I joined the Missionary Baptist church. Those were tough times, but during those days I defied any man to beat me to the draw. While working on the scout gang, I rode for Buffalo Bill on his ranch at North Platte, Nebraska. It was here where I later on rode the Black Diamond mare in the open prairie. No one else had ridden her in the open before."

"In the spring of '88 I joined the Pinkerton detectives. That fall I joined the Anti-Horse Thief Association to clear Texas of horse thieves. We rode up and down the Red River, in east Texas, and Indian Territory. We rode up the Ozark Trail in Missouri before we quit. I investigated many cases of counter branding. Several times, with some quick shooting, I shot the branding iron from the hands of the thief."

"Judge Parker, a United States judge at Fort Smith, Arkansas, asked me to go into the Ozark Mountains to pick up the many gangs of thieves operating there. He offered me twenty-five men. I refused, telling him, 'Those men know their hills and hideouts too well.' I told him it would be suicide, but to wait until spring when the thieves came out of hiding with their stolen horses. It took us four years to break them up. All the offenses committed in Indian Territory were tried by Old Judge Parker at Fort Smith. I was well acquainted with him."

"Going over in the Creek Nation to Round Top Mountain, in '88, we were invited to a big dance, to which we went. We were looking for stolen horses. It was a regular outlaw dance, I'd call it. A fight started that night. Al Jennings and some others rode out. Four men were killed and seven were wounded. When the shooting started in the house, I saw I couldn't get out, so I just laid down on the floor. About the time the shooting ceased, a man came in and turned me over, saying, 'Did I get you Tony? If I knew I didn't, I'd finish you up.' I said nothing and played dead. He thought I was Tony McClure, a deputy marshal. I got up and went out of the house and started to get some water from the well, running over two wounded men. The first thing a wounded man wants is water. So I went to the well and filled my hat with water. I began to give it to them. Jack Shaw, Tony McClure, and Ozark Jack were all shot up pretty bad. Ozark Jack is still living. I saw him about a year ago. We went down to the ravine, got our horses, and pulled back to the Chickasaw Nation."

"I joined the U.S. Marshal's force in '92. During the time I was a deputy marshal I saw six train holdups. We saved three of them from losing any money. The Daltons held up a train in the spring of '92. I think it was in the spring. They killed a deputy who failed to put them up fast enough. One of them looked at me and said, 'We know who you are. Put 'em up or I'll kill you.' I put 'em up, too, I did."

"When this judge asked why we let them get away, I told him I knew the Daltons and I didn't want to fight them alone, either. We all put up our hands except one man, and he is buried out there, too."

"Cherokee Bill's gang held up a train. Joe Shaw's boys got one too. Joe was a good safe-cracker. They didn't get anything. Al Jennings held up a train. They didn't get much. There were four bank holdups and we saved two of them."

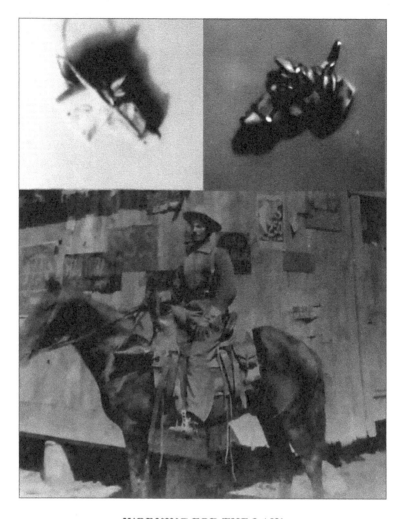

WORKING FOR THE LAW
Bill Roberts while serving on the U.S. Marshal's force, age about thirty. The small photographs are of his Anti-Horse Thief badge, made of bone laced with yellow gold wire. Note the C branded under the mane of the animals belonging to members of the Association

"I was with the bunch that took Robber's Roost. Also I was in the bunch that captured Crazy Snake, the Indian. We chased them into the mountains, where they hid. Their boys brought food to them. A marshal named Jones roped one of the boys and hung him to a tree till he was glad to tell us where the Indians were hiding. After a brief trial the court turned them loose."

"In the fall of '88 there was staged a cowboy roundup in Cheyenne. The judges wanted me to enter the contest riding a horse known as Cyclone. I didn't have the entry fee. I rode horses of every make, breed, and color on every ranch in the state till I was really saddle toughened. Then I knew I was ready for old Cyclone. So, in '89, I returned to the roundup. Tom Waggoner covered all the bets and I won the championship riding Cyclone, and Tom gave me $10,000 for winning for him. I was known as the Hugo Kid."

"We went to Oklahoma City for the winter. In January, 1890, Indian Jim sent me to a boxing school in Cincinnati, Ohio, where I trained. I was tired of riding outlaw horses and thought I would like to be a boxer. I was left-handed and fast, but they put me in the ring with a long-armed fellow and I decided that my arms were too short to continue boxing. I went back to Oklahoma City and rode horses again in spare time. We kept riding the anti-horse-thief trail."

"I rode Crazy Fox in Old Mexico. Crazy Fox was a buckskin with a black stripe down his back and black stripes around his legs. He weighed about a thousand pounds and was well built, about eight years old, with a ewe neck and a Roman nose, and it looked as if both his eyes came out the same place. I contested him according to

Cheyenne rules. He pitched like a mountain horse, only worse while it lasted, but not so long. Pitching about three hundred yards, he broke into a run. Jim roped him, and they didn't want to pay off. They finally paid up, and we went to Fort Worth, Texas. After that I went to Sulphur Springs, where I rode Lone Wolf in Booger Red's show. We went on to Cold Creek, Idaho, where I rode Wild Cat in the summer of '92. In the fall I rode the Black Diamond mare at Buffalo Bill's ranch on North Platte. Then I rode Wild Hyena at Pendleton, Oregon, Smokey at the Diamond A, and Man Killer in Cheyenne."

"In 1893, my riding skill gave me a trip to the Argentine Republic. A company had shipped a large bunch of Western horses down there. The natives couldn't do anything with them. The Cattleman's Association sent me and Indian Jim there to break the horses. We left Oklahoma City about the tenth of January, 1893, and sailed to Buenos Aires. For the first few days we looked around to see the brands on the horses so we could tell where they were from. We found quite a few Wyoming horses in the herd."

"I was supposed to ride four horses a day, two in the morning and two in the afternoon. After we taught them how to ride, we showed them how to drive the horses. I would ride four one day and they would take them the next day, and so on. After we were there some six months, they suggested that we have a contest ride. We held a contest for three days, riding horses and steers, and bulldogging and roping just like we did in the United States. On the third day I rode Zebra Dun."

"Zebra Dun was an outlaw when he was shipped there. I asked them to raise a bet and I'd ride him. I told them I was supposed to ride him anyway, but would like to have it sweetened. After I stepped off, I put a bridle on him and hopped on and rode him with a bridle. I had taught them to ride in the slick and to ride with a surcingle. Now they wanted me to ride him with a surcingle, which I did."

"Sometime in 1894 we contracted to go to the Shetland Islands to catch ponies. They were hard to rope in that brush. They would run like rabbits. We spent about three months catching some 150 head of ponies. When we came back we joined up again with the Anti-Horse Thief Association in Indian Territory. They put us on the North Canadian River."

"One morning Mountain Bill and I were riding along when a shot struck him from across the river. He fell off the horse, wounded. I drew my rifle from the scabbard. Taking my field glasses, I spied a Creek Indian across the river. I fired four shots. He never showed up any more. I put Bill on his horse and took him to a cow ranch some ten miles away. We shipped him to Ardmore, where he died from the wound. I wrote to his sister in Arizona and his brother-in-law came and got his belongings. I made a report of all this and they signed me up with a fellow named Boyles."

"In the fall of '94 I went back on the marshal force and served three more years. I would take off a couple of months each year and ride with Buffalo Bill's and Pawnee Bill's Wild West shows."

"In '95 I struck out for El Paso, where I run into a bunch of cowboys with whom I was acquainted. They said it was a good time to put up a ranch in Old Mexico, as Old Diaz had offered good terms on the grazing land. By paying a small fee, you could graze all the land you needed. It looked like a good proposition. Ten of us agreed to put up a ranch over there, with not more than ten shares to each man. We bought about a thousand cattle and fifty pony mares. We fixed up everything and appointed a boss. I decided to put Jim in my place and I went back to Indian Territory. Late in the fall I went back to Mexico, arriving about Christmas at the ranch. I was still called Hugo Kid here. We ranched through the years of '96 and '97, raising mules and steel-dust horses."

"In the spring of '98 Roosevelt called for volunteers for his regiment of Rough Riders. Jim and I were in Claremore about this time, so we went to Muskogee and enlisted."

"They transferred us to San Antonio, where we stayed about three weeks before we started for Cuba. We went through Mobile, Alabama, where they gave us a midnight supper. It was not long until we landed in Cuba. A lieutenant by the name of Cook stepped up to me and said, 'Ain't this the Texas Kid?' I told him it was, and he said, 'You'd make a good scout. You were good in Indian Territory scouting horse thieves. We will take you and the Cherokee Indian for scouts."

"They put from one to fifteen on a scout gang and they would hunt the enemy out and report back to headquarters. I told Jim that we had put ourselves up as another target. I followed that about two months, seeing scouts shot on every side of me. Jim and I always made it out."

"They shipped lots of Western ponies down there, and there were lots of them that the boys couldn't ride. Cook to them he could get them a man that could ride them. So they sent for me and the Indian to come down to the corral. I saddled up one and kicked him out like I'd always rode. They said they would give me a job riding them. I told them I wanted Jim for my helper. I thought this was better than being shot from ambush."

"In a little while I had charge of these horses. Some of the officers didn't like this and I told them to take off their stripes, which they did, and we proved our manhood. In about four days I whipped two of them, but still held my job. The officers treated lots of the boys very mean."

"During a battle one day there were four officers shot in the back. They thought that some of us and the Cherokee Indian did it, which they tried to prove in court-martial, but failed. When our time was out they gave us a bobtailed discharge. I didn't think I was entitled to it, because they did not prove anything on me."

"We mustered out, coming back to the U. S. Jim and I went back to Mexico on the ranch. In June, 1899, Old Diaz seized everything. They would not let us ship or drive our cattle out of there. They sent soldiers down to drive our stuff off. We asked for thirty days grace. We thought we might get some help from the U.S. If not, we could get some ammunition."

"About fifty soldiers came there to round up our cattle and horses. We sent an interpreter down to talk to them. They said it was Diaz' orders. We had thirty-six cowboys. We fired into them with .3o-3o rifles and picked them off like blackbirds. The fourth morning when we got up, we were surrounded by almost two thousand soldiers. I climbed up on the barn and tacked up a red blanket."

"Each man packed his horse like he was going off for a ride. We agreed to fire into them in the weakest spot, then make our getaway if we could. We fought for twelve days, living on wild game and trying to escape into the U.S. On the thirteenth morning we crossed the Rio Grande below Del Rio. I had a cousin there on the Ranger force. He helped us with food. I was supposed to be worth about thirty thousand dollars, but came out with one horse and saddle."

"In the spring of 1902, I started a Wild West show which I operated until 1904. Then I went to Canton, in Van Zandt County. From Canton I went into Indian Territory, trading horses and cattle."

"I went back to Mexico about 1907 and three of us started another ranch known as the Three Bar. In 1910 the revolution came along, and we had to start fighting again. We joined with Carranza's men, and later with Pancho Villa. I was captain of 106 men, all mounted on steeldust horses from our ranch. Our steeldust horses could outdistance the Spanish ponies of the Federals. We left Mexico in 1914, coming across the border at Brownsville, Texas. The Mexican revolution broke us up. We lost everything we had, about $200,000 between the three of us."

"In 1912 I met Mollie Brown of Coleman, Texas, and we were married. She was a member of the old Brown family, of Brownwood, Texas. We went back to east Texas and then into Oklahoma, in the trading business again. Later on I had a ranch in Arkansas, near Oklahoma. I kept on riding bucking horses and doing about anything I could find to do. I worked in the oil fields of Oklahoma. When oil was struck in east Texas, I went to Gladewater. I worked for the city of Gladewater as a plainclothesman. I aided Green, the Chief of Police. It was here that I took part in breaking up a gang of bank robbers holed up in the Sabine River bottom."

"Molly died in 1919. I married Louticia Ballard in 1925, with whom I lived until her death in 1944. Then I married Melinda Allison, in November, 1944."

That brought Brushy Bill up to date. He had little to be proud of at the end. He was old and poor, and just another old character to most people. He had memories, but he couldn't talk about the ones that meant most to him—not until he decided to "come out," and then they were beginning to fade."

He commented to Morrison on the difficulty of bringing those far-off events into focus: "Sixty-nine years is a long time to recollect some of those things. I never forgot some. I'll never forget that trial at Mesilla . . . the fight at Blazer's. He was pouring it on us. Got Brewer too. Almost got me . . . McSween's house burning . . . my jail break when I killed them two guards . . . that fight with Garrett's posse at that rock house on Christmas. The reason I can't forget about some of those times is that I was fighting for my life. You wouldn't forget about them either, would you?"

"All these years I have been running and hiding when I knew I wasn't wrong. But I had to hide. Been thinking about it more since I don't have long here anymore. I want to get straightened out before I die, I do. I've been a good useful citizen and I think I deserve a break. If we have to go to court I can still tell 'em a few things. That Ring bunch was terrible. I'm not afraid to talk if you don't let them lock me up."

"Sixty-nine years is a long time to recollect, my friend."

STILL ABOVE GROUND IN 1950?
Brushy Bill Roberts beside the grave of Billy the Kid. Snapshot taken July 6, 1950, at Fort Sumner, New Mexico

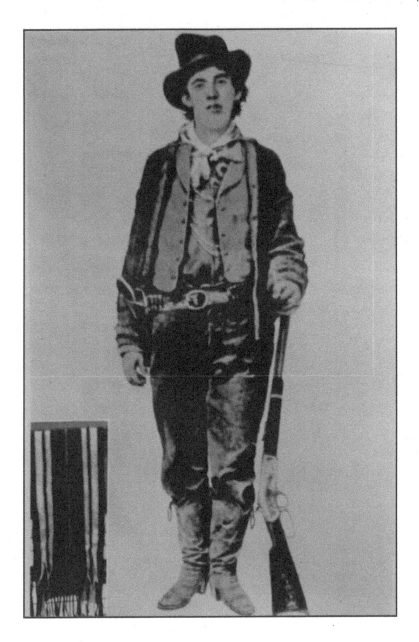

THE TINTYPE AND DELUVINA'S SCARF
Billy traded the tintype for the multicolored angora wool scarf woven by Deluvina
Maxwell and wore it about his head on his way to jail

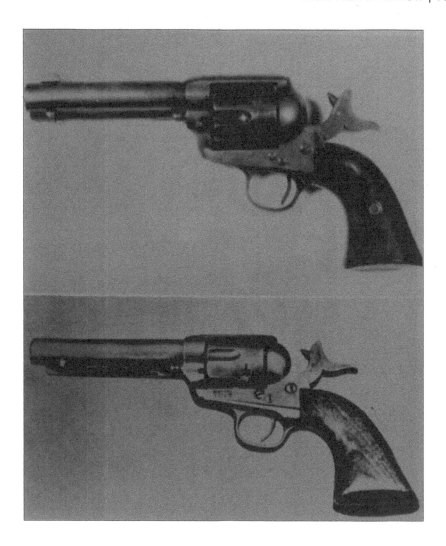

TWO .44'S

At the top is the six-shooter carried by Bill Roberts from the nineties until his death- a Colt's single-action Frontier Model, serial number 176903. At the bottom is the weapon taken from Billy the Kid when he surrendered to Garrett- a Colt's single-action Frontier Model, serial number 0361, made in 1874. These revolvers were chambered to fire rifle ammunition

THE OLD COURTHOUSE
Taken about 1884
The man on the extreme left is John W. Poe

A STUDY IN EARS
Brushy Bill Roberts at fourteen [inset] (photography made at Fort Smith, Arkansas); at seventeen [top, left] (taken, according to his story, at Dodge City with the Jones brothers); at twenty-seven [lower left] (crayon portrait made at Butte, Montana); at fifty-five [top right] (Brownville, Texas); and at eighty-five [lower right] (Hamilton, Texas). Note the protruding left ear

CHAPTER EIGHT
_____

THE TANGLED WEB

BRUSHY BILL was a hard man to back track. He had wandered over many lands, had used a dozen aliases, and had covered his trail wherever he could. He had, in fact, spent seventy years making it hard to believe that he could be anybody but Brushy Bill Roberts.

He was resentful of any attempt to pin a Billy the Kid label on him. He once wrote to Morrison about an Oklahoma woman who wanted to write him up: "She said she had three affidavits that people knew me in 1887. . . . These men said I was Billie the Kid. I told her she thinks she caught a sucker. I ain't putting out nothing. . . . I don't like for other people to meddle with my business."

In various ways he tried to lay false scents. One was by writing up his history the way he wanted it told. He set down his story in a series of paper-covered composition books—the kind schoolboys use for their class exercises—and in a couple of loose-leaf notebooks. One of the latter is dated 1925. He started over two or three times and told the tale approximately the same way in each case.

It is a wild and woolly narrative. He pictures himself as traveling all over the West making a living riding outlaw horses, serving as a frontier peace officer, working for the Anti-Horse Thief organization in Oklahoma, running a traveling rodeo show, soldiering, and ranching. He makes his age out to be eight years less than it would have been if he fought in the Lincoln County feud, and telescopes events that happened in the seventies with others that must have occurred in the eighties and nineties. Much of it may be fiction. It is impossible about now to say how much of it is true, and it would take years and a lot of money to find out.

One fact hits the reader between the eyes at once: there is not one single reference to Lincoln County, Billy the Kid, Pat Garrett, or anything else that might connect Brushy Bill Roberts with the cattle troubles in New Mexico. In fact, the author never places himself closer to the Ruidoso country than the Diamond A ranch, many miles to the west.

This is almost enough to make a skeptic laugh Brushy Bill out of court. But then comes the thought that the complete omission of all such detail might be highly significant. Brushy Bill certainly knew plenty about New Mexico troubles and the people who fought in them. He must have been on the inside somehow, Why should he have passed this chapter over completely unless he had something to conceal?

There is a possibility that he did write down some of the things he was trying to hide. Three of his notebooks have disappeared; Morrison had a brief look at them, but the old man would not allow him to make a real examination or to take many notes. After his death, Morrison and Mrs. Roberts looked for those books and could not find them. Morrison thinks Bill destroyed them just before he left for his disastrous interview with the governor in Santa Fe, thinking they might be incriminating evidence if he should be arrested and sent to jail, as he feared he might be.

There is some reason to believe that he spent all his mature life impersonating one of his own relatives. This was the real Ollie Roberts, a cousin, who was born in 1867, ran away from home about 1884, and was killed in the Indian Territory in a difficulty about some stolen horses.

As Brushy Bill told it, he and his side-kick, Indian Jim, were scouting for stolen stock one time and reached a community named Shakerag, here they expected to pick up some contraband horses. The deputy sheriff at this place reported that he had killed two men who were in possession of the animals, and they all went out to bury the bodies.

The deputy searched the dead men, appropriated their money and personal effects, and was going on with the burying when Bill recognized one of the victims as his cousin Ollie. He looked under the mane of one of the horses and found the brand of the Anti-Horse Thief Association, realized that his cousin was working for the law, and stopped the proceedings at once. "We know this man," he said to the deputy. "He ain't no horse thief."

Using his leverage as an officer, he took over his cousin's belongings, intending to return them to the boy's family. He probably hung onto them, however, for when he finally located the survivors at Sulphur Springs, Texas, they took him for the runaway boy and he let them think he was.

Dudley Heath, who was married to Billy's cousin Martha, was dubious. "That's not your brother," he told her. But Ollie's mother took Brushy Bill to her bosom as a long-lost son, and members of the family, down through the years, called him Ollie and supposed he was the son of the woman who claimed him. When the time came to straighten the record out, there were many difficulties. Brushy Bill often had his doubts about going through with it, and he hated to own up to a good many things he supposedly had done. He would grow red in the face and object violently: "Now you're trying to get me to admit I did that, and I won't do it. I won't admit it!"

Morrison would fuss back at him, "Do you want me to take this case or not? If you don't I'll take my hat and walk right out of that door. How do you expect me to do anything for you if you won't talk?"

And the old man would look sheepish and try to be frank.

Morrison got some of it on his tape recorder, and more of it in his notes, but he had to be careful. The sight of pencil and paper made Roberts uneasy, and sometimes he would shut up like a clam when Morrison began to scribble. When he did get strung out he told whatever came into his head, seldom following a straight line of narrative, and his story, as set down in these pages had to be assembled from various interviews where he added details about this or that episode.

Morrison planned to go over all of it with him as soon as Governor Mabry acted favorably on the application for pardon. But then the whole show went to pieces. Mabry refused to act. The old man died. Nothing further could be done.

In one interview Bill talked at some length about the people who knew, or had known, who he was, and about the trouble he had in keeping under cover. Buffalo Bill, he said, had been acquainted with Wild Henry

Roberts and was aware of the identity of Henry's son. Pawnee Bill was another who knew, and there is some evidence to support this contention. In 1938, the newspapers picked up a story from the Associated Press that Pawnee Bill and a group of friends were laying plans to visit the Southwest in search of Billy the Kid, whom they believed to be still alive.

GOVERNOR THOMAS J. MABRY

Tom Waggoner, who backed Brushy Bill as a bronc rider at Cheyenne in 1889, knew whom he was backing, according to Brushy Bill.

Judge Parker, of Fort Smith, Arkansas, told Bill he knew who he was when he came up for appointment as Deputy United States Marshal, and at first said he would "have no goddam outlaws working for him." However, he changed his mind.

Bill went on to tell about a good many more:

"A lot of dead men in those days showed up in Old Mexico later on. They would leave Texas for New Mexico. Then from here they would go to Old Mexico or California. A lot of them never left New Mexico because they never got caught. Longwell went to El Paso and opened up a stable. I saw lots of him after I went into Old Mexico. He knew Garrett did not kill me. He knew George Cole, who I stayed with sometimes in El Paso after that killing in Fort Sumner. They knew Tex Moore, too. Tex worked for Chisum but he was not in that war. Tex knows who I am too, he does. John Selman knew Garrett didn't kill me. I saw Selman at Cole's saloon in El Paso in the 90's. He was afraid to say anything, though. He followed me outside and we talked. He had no use for Garrett. Almost killed Garrett in the Panhandle before the Lincoln County War. He said Garrett killed a man that did not need killing. I had helped Selman when he needed help and he was ready to help me now. But I wasn't ready to come out yet."

"I started to come clean when that revolution broke out there in Old Mexico. I talked to a lawyer in El Paso about it, but I lost everything in that Mexican war. Come out with one horse and riding rig. Didn't intend to make myself known after that. They would not have let me alone if I'd come out that time. I didn't want no more trouble, so I just lived Brushy Bill, that's all."

"I got around and talked to some of the boys until I got too old to run around. I was accused of being Billy the Kid from Montana to Missouri, but I denied it, saying I never knew Billy the Kid, that I was too young. I looked younger than I really was all through my lifetime. Then again I had to tell some of them, "If you know who I am, you will keep your mouth shut." These little feet, little hands with large wrists, standing so straight, talking and laughing all the time, would give me away when I was around anyone who had known Billy the Kid."

"There have been lots of them said they knew Billy the Kid, but they didn't, they didn't. They just thought they had known him. There were lots of them looking for Billy the Kid until he showed up. Then they changed their minds. Captain Hughes and Captain McDonald were my friends. They didn't know I was the Kid. That was before their time. They thought Garrett had killed the Kid. It made me mad, it did. I told Captain Hughes Garrett didn't kill him—that I had seen him in South America in '93."

"I saw Brown in '82, but he didn't want anyone to know about it. Brown and Jesse Evans knew that Garrett didn't kill the Kid. I helped Jesse with money after I was on the marshal force. Tom Pickett too. I run into Tom in Arizona. I don't remember where, but Jim and I were on the trail of a man. We went through New Mexico about '92 after a man. That is when I talked to George Coe over there. He was scared to death when I walked up to talk to him. He told me to get out of the country, that a lot of my enemies were still around. He had left the country at the time I was supposed to be killed, but he was told I was killed by Garrett. I saw him again sometime in the early 1900's. He knew I was ranching in Old Mexico too."

"I was in Albuquerque and Santa Fe in the late 90's and 1900s early. I came to El Paso all through the years. I never saw Rudabaugh after that war in Mexico. I saw Pickett, though, after that. Yes, quite a while after that."

CHAPTER NINE

BE HE ALIVE OR BE HE DEAD

THE MOST ticklish part of Brushy Bill's case was the process of locating and interviewing old-timers who could and would say yes or no to his claim. The whole thing was complicated by the fact that Billy the Kid had become a legend, even in the minds of those who had known him. Stories about the Kid's death or survival had been current for so long and had been argued over so often that practically all interested persons had their minds already made up. Some were ready to maintain with firmness, and even with fury, that Billy was absolutely dead and positively buried. A much smaller group was unalterably convinced that this was not so, and they knew it.

Strangely enough, the ones who had the most deeply rooted doubts about Billy's demise were not necessarily outsiders who had steeped themselves in The Saga of Billy the Kid. They were likely to be real old-timers, or people who had known the Lincoln country for a long time.

The rumor that Billy had survived was current at the time of his supposed demise. Mrs. J. H. Wood, whose husband was a rancher and blacksmith at Seven Rivers, maintained to the day of her death that Billy ate dinner at her house three days after he was supposed to have been killed. And there were others.

Among the letters which Morrison received when he announced in the newspapers that he wished to make contact with people who had known Billy the Kid, was one from Mrs. W. W. Carson, of San Angelo, Texas, dated November 29, 1950. "I lived in the Penasco country for 2 years, she wrote, "from October, 1887, to October, 1889. It was rumored then that 'Billie' was in hiding in the mountains there."

"In the spring of '88 or '89, I was returning to my school on Lower Peliasco, riding horseback. Couldn't get my pony to get into the water to cross the river. After quite a while of useless attempt, a young man suddenly appeared from nowhere and asked if he could assist me. He led the horse or pony across the wide expanse of that river. When I described, him to many of the old timers they all said it was Billie the Kid.—He was supposed to have been dead a few years previous but those in the Peliasco region did not believe him to be dead. . . . I recall that he was very kind to a young scared girl school teacher and was a perfect gentleman."

Similar testimony came from Arthur Hyde, of the Veterans' Hospital at Whipple, Arizona. He told of a visit he paid, in 1914, to Mr. Goforth, a relative who had lived since 1900 at the head of the Mimbres River. Goforth sent him to an old-timer named Thompson, late of the Sacramento country, when the subject of Billy the Kid came up. Thompson was convinced that Garrett and Billy had cooked up a scheme to make it look as if Garrett had lived up to his campaign promises—which included getting rid of the Kid. A Mexican boy turned up who looked something like Billy and could be used as a substitute.

"Garrett told the young Mexican to go to the Maxwell house where he would meet a rancher who might give him a job. The rest of the episode went off just as it had been written over time and again. They had a quiet burial on the grounds lest some of his followers might cause trouble and the casket was not opened at the burial. Mr. Thompson told us he had heard that Billy went to the state of Chihuahua, Mexico, and went into ranching. . . . "

"As it happened, I got t.b. in the service and was sent to the old army hospital at Fort Bayard, near Silver City, New Mexico, for treatment. After I got discharged early in 1920 I spent the next four years rambling around in the Mogollons and the Black Range. I met up with several old-timers who told me just about the same story. Among them was a Mr. J.E. George (now dead) at Mule Creek and a Bill Jones, also dead, at Reserve, New Mexico. They all told me it was just a case of dirty-rotten politics, and Billy just happened to serve their purpose. They didn't seem to consider the killing of the innocent Mexican of any importance. Judging from what they told me it was common knowledge among those who were on the inside at the time."

The undercurrents of gossip which carried rumors such as these sometimes allowed a piece of conversational driftwood to come to the surface. Over and over again, as the years went by, the newspapers would discover that Billy was rumored to be alive, would print a story about it, and then run for cover as attackers and defenders closed in from all sides.

One such tidbit appeared in the El Paso Herald for June 23, 1926. Someone had heard something at Alamogordo, New Mexico: "The story that Billy the Kid was not killed by Pat Garrett in 1881, but that he was seen as late as 1910, did not come as a complete surprise in this section for old men in the Lincoln vicinity have never conceded the Kid's death. George Coe, of Glencoe, a side partner of Billy the Kid and one of the two survivors of the Kid's faction has declared many times that he did not believe that the Kid was killed."

"C. C. McNatt, of Alamogordo, was in the vicinity of Lincoln when the Kid was supposed to have been killed, and he recalls that the settlers there at the time doubted the story of the Kid's death. Many believed it was a frame-up between those who wanted the reward, and Billy, who had served his purpose in breaking up the cattle ring and was willing to leave."

So it went. Billy's ghost walked again—in 1937 when Pawnee Bill and some of his friends advertised an intention to search for Billy the Kid somewhere in the Southwest—again in 1948 when an old prospector named Manuel Taylor told a strange tale to Mr. L.S. Cardwell, of Las Cruces. Mrs. Cardwell was a special writer for the El Paso Times, and sent the story in.

"I knew Billy the Kid well when he was at Silver City," Taylor declared. "We used to run horse races together. In fact another young fellow and myself once pried the bars off the chimney top at the old adobe jail so that Billy could climb out."

"The man killed at Maxwell's was a young cattle detective who had come in from the East and expected to make some easy money capturing cattle rustlers and 'got his' by mistake...."

"I was in Guadalajara, Mexico, in 1914 where I met the Kid. The recognition was mutual and we had a few drinks together for old time's sake. He has married there and has a family. Cardwell stopped off at Hillsboro, New Mexico, and "took the trouble to inquire regarding Manuel Taylor and was told that he was well known there and was known to be truthful and trustworthy."

A good running summary of the ebb and flow of the underground currents is provided by John J. Clancy, now of Neihart, Montana, but for many years a resident of eastern New Mexico: "In passing, I might say that in the 1930's there arose a big controversy over whether the Kid had really been killed by Garrett or not. Some fellow up and said he had seen the Kid somewhere in California running some kind of restaurant. Another said he had seen him in Old Mexico. Somebody over in Mora County, a close Anglo-American friend of the Kid's, claimed he had seen the Kid a couple of weeks after he was alleged to have been killed, over in his country. Then the late Jim Abercrombie, daring adventurer in his own right, late pioneer merchant of Anton Chico, N. M., claimed he had seen the Kid, had been with him after his alleged 'taking hence' at Fort Sumner, N. M., by Pat Garrett. The story went round with the usual heated pros and cons back and forth, but finally petered out.

Even Burns, author of the Saga of the Kid, came to the rescue with a rather high-falutin' comeback. The latest revival of this claim was a couple of months ago when someone claimed that the real Kid was up to then living at Duncan, Arizona; that he was an old man, of course, quite pleasant of character and talked of things quite intelligently. This summer, when I was at Santa Rosa, N. M., a telegraph operator named Thomas told me casually that he knew this "Kid man and confirmed quite well what I had already heard about him."

Such stories, of course, establish nothing more than the fact that many people chose to believe the old folk story that keeps every outlaw hero alive—a story which would naturally retain its vitality in a region where even the school children are said to cherish the old partisanships.

But it is harder to get around the fact that some of Billy's very closest friends are reported, on good authority, to have doubted the fact of his death. Higinio Salazar was mentioned in 1933 as one who had his doubts.

Newspaper stories involving George Coe have already been mentioned, though in fairness it should be admitted that George accepted the usual version of the Kid's death in his autobiography Frontier Fighter, and many of his friends and relatives insist that the book expresses his real opinion. His cousin, Frank Coe, seems to have had a strong feeling that the Kid might still be above ground.

Frank's daughter, Mrs. Helena LeMay, told Morrison that he always investigated reports that Billy was alive. Once he heard that his old friend was living in California. He took the family with him and went out to see about it. He left them in the car while he paid a visit to the claimant, who was living in a shack on the outskirts of a California town. He came back disappointed, and with tears in his eyes, saying that the man was an impostor.

OLD FORT SUMNER
Company Quarters from the Old Sutler's Store

With this background of contention and counter-contention, Morrison had his difficulties when it came time to gather testimony which would establish the identity of his man. After so many false alarms, people were mighty touchy—afraid of making themselves ridiculous—afraid of causing trouble and argument in their communities. Nevertheless the job had to be done, and during the month of April, 1950, Morrison and Brushy Bill went on pilgrimage to interview as many old settlers as possible.

One of their best prospects was Severo Gallegos, of Ruidoso, New Mexico. He was the boy who was playing marbles under the tree in Lincoln while Billy the Kid shot Bell and Olinger, and who got the outlaw a rope just before he rode away. This is Morrison's account of the conversations with Mr. Gallegos:

"Upon arriving in Ruidoso, I visited with Mr. Gallegos. While talking to him, I told him that I had an old friend in my room that I would like him to meet. At my room I introduced my friend as William H. Bonney. Mr. Gallegos seemed spellbound as he looked at and talked to Billy. They talked about happenings there during the days of Billy the Kid. After several hours of visiting, he was still somewhat skeptical, but thought it might be Billy the Kid. He would not commit himself without some more positive identification. I took him home late that night. He wanted to talk to him the next morning before we left Ruidoso."

"The next morning I arrived at the Gallegos home late. He was waiting to talk to me. His first remark was: 'Your man talks like Billy; he looks like Billy; he has small hands and large wrists, small feet, large ears, stands and walks like Billy; but he is not old enough to be Billy the Kid."

"I told him that I would not take him back just out of curiosity, but if he thought he might be able to identify my friend, I would let them visit again. I knew Billy was peculiar, and that he wanted no publicity."

"Mr. Gallegos said, 'If I could look into his eyes, I could tell for sure if he was really Billy. Billy had small brown spots in the blue of his eyes. If your man has these same kind of spots, I will say that he is Billy the Kid."

"I was very familiar with my man, but I had never noticed the spots in his eyes. I thought it only fair that Mr. Gallegos have another chance to view Billy and find out for himself whether or not he was really Billy the Kid."

"When we arrived at my room, I stepped inside and asked Billy to open the Venetian blind and stand in the light of the window so that Mr. Gallegos would have an opportunity to see for himself in daylight. Billy stepped up as directed. Mr. Gallegos looked very carefully, then remarked: 'That is Billy the Kid, all right. Only Billy has eyes like that. I am ready to swear that this man is Billy the Kid."

An affidavit of identification was executed before a notary public.

Morrison and Brushy Bill went back to El Paso, where there were more old-timers to see. Luis Martinez, of Parral, Mexico, and Hernando Chavez, of Torreon, stated that to their knowledge Billy the Kid had lived in Mexico after his supposed death. "We were told," said Chavez, "that Billy the Kid fought with Carranza and Pancho Villa during the Revolution."

After that they went calling on one of Billy the Kid's old acquaintances—Mrs. Martile Able, widow of John Able. Both she and her husband had been Billy's friends.

Mrs. Able was eighty-nine years old at the time of the interview, and bedfast, but she was sure. To an El Paso reporter she delivered herself as follows: "I knew him the moment I saw him. He is alive. Others have tried to impersonate him, but the man I talked to in July was the real Billy. A long time ago a man was brought before me as Billy the Kid, but he wasn't. He was a faker."

"But I recognized this Billy because I know him well."

"I had not seen Billy since before Pat Garrett claimed he shot him."

"When Billy's lawyer, William V. Morrison, of St. Louis, brought Billy to the home of my grandson in the Lower Valley, he asked Billy, "Do you know this lady?""

"And Billy said, 'Sure, that's John Able's wife.""

"Would a faker know my husband, John, or remember me?""

"Many times Billy would come to our house when he was on the dodge. My husband would give him horses and would be on the lookout while Billy was eating. When he came to see me he still had his gun and pocket-knife that he always carried. I would never forget them because I saw them many times.'"

Mrs. Able did not hesitate to sign an affidavit that Brushy Bill Roberts was Billy the Kid.

On July 2, Morrison and Bill started on a final jaunt through the Lincoln country. Their first stop was Carlsbad, where they had arranged to meet Sam Jones and his older brother, William Jones. Sam was living in Carlsbad, but Bill was still operating on the old ranch in Rocky Arroyo—the same ranch Billy the Kid had stumbled into when he lost his horse in the Guadalupe Mountains in 1877. They were brothers of John and Jim Jones, who worked with the Kid at Chisum's ranch and fought in the cattle war.

The three old men had a long talk together and Morrison was certain that they would help his cause along with the affidavits he wanted, but he was disappointed. William Shafer, Bill Jones' grandson, wrote on July 9, 1950: "I am sorry, but Mr. Jones does not feel that he can sign your affidavits that your man is Billy the Kid. He gave no conclusive proof of this at the time we met him. It seems to me that if he were Billy the Kid, he would not need affidavits to prove his contention. He would just be Billy the Kid."

Sam Jones wrote, "Received your letter, and am sorry but feel that I can't sign the affidavit. I'm old and I just don't feel like being obligated so."

They had better luck at Carrizozo, where they stopped the day after visiting the Jones brothers. They went to see Jose B. Montoya, who had previously told Morrison that he had seen Billy the Kid at a bullfight in Juarez in 1902. He knew it was Billy, he said, because he had been a schoolboy in Lincoln during the time that Billy was there. His people lived on a ranch in the Capitan Mountains, and Billy sometimes stayed there. After the escape from the Lincoln jail, Montoya did not see the Kid again until 1902, when he ran into him in Juarez. "He was wearing a large hat and a buckskin jacket. Alfred Green and I were there. Both of us knew

Billy. Alfred was older and he really knew Billy well. He was talking to a couple of Mexican officers. We looked for him after the bullfight but couldn't locate him."

Morrison introduced Brushy Bill to Montoya, and they talked for a while. Finally Montoya said, "By golly, that's Billy and I am ready to swear that it is him." They looked up a notary and he signed an affidavit.

The next stop was Hot Springs, now Truth or Consequences, where Morrison took up the trail of Manuel Taylor—the same Manuel Taylor who had told his tale to L. A. Cardwell, in 1948. Senator Burton Roach had once employed him and was able to pass on the disappointing intelligence that Manuel was dead."

They went on to Albuquerque and Santa Fe. In neither town where they able to find anyone who had actually known Billy the Kid, but they had some interesting conversations. As they passed the Governor's Palace in Santa Fe, Bill remarked, "Now right here is where I crossed the street on the way back to the jail down there (pointing westward). I was handcuffed and leg ironed always. Sometimes they would bring me up here at noon time and keep me here all afternoon so people could come and make fun of me. I had to hobble over stones down there to the adobe jail. Those leg irons and chains would get heavy before I got there. They walked me every place.

"I spent some bad times in this old town, and some good ones too. Used to have big affairs here—dances...."

"Here is where the governor double-crossed me, too. He

wouldn't come down to the jail here and talk to me. He was glad to come down to Patron's when I was locked up in Lincoln that time, because he needed my help then. But he forgot how I helped him and wouldn't come down here to talk to me. He thought I was helpless and they were going to hang me.

"That governor didn't treat me right, he didn't. This governor here now ought to help me, since the other one promised to pardon me, don't you think so?"

Morrison thought so.

They went on to Las Vegas—where nobody was left who knew Billy—and on to Fort Sumner, where Brushy Bill boarded the train for Texas.

So it went, with success and failure intermingled. Bill had said Tex Moore, the cowboy artist at Wichita Falls, knew who he was and would testify. Morrison wrote just after Mr. Moore fell into his last illness, and was never able to arrange an interview. But DeWitt Travis, a Longview, Texas, oil man, wrote that he had known Bill from his own boyhood and had always been certain that he was Billy the Kid. He signed an affidavit and wrote to Morrison: "My father, Elbert Travis, and Brushy Bill's father served together under Quantrill during the Civil War. My mother, Martha Ann Patterson, and Brushy Bill's mother were girlhood friends—in fact, friends through life. With this background I have known Brushy Bill intimately all my life."

DeWitt Travis could give circumstantial answers to Morrison's questions, for instance, one about Billy the Kid's teeth—those famous teeth. On January 23, 1951, he wrote: "About Bill's teeth—the two eye teeth were so very big until they looked like tushes—when he lost several of his under or lower teeth, they bothered him an awful lot so he had a Dr. Cruz in Gladewater take them out—Dr. Cruz died about six years ago. Taking Bill's teeth out made him a lot harder to identify. Bill was a better looking man after his teeth were taken out than he was before—for they really ruined his looks."

Scraps of information accumulated to bolster Morrison's conviction that he was on the right track. He interviewed one pioneer woman, whose name he promised not to mention, at San Patricio, New Mexico. Among the questions he put to her, writing them down since she was too deaf to hear, was one asking if Billy had ever owned a house in San Patricio. Brushy Bill had said he did. The books make him out a homeless drifter. The old lady swung her hand out toward the hills across the way and said, "Yes he did. Right over there where that road is now. He used to live over there when he was in town."

Even Brushy Bill's wife, though she was supposed to have been kept in ignorance, contributed a touching little interview which Morrison captured on a tape recorder.

"Of course you didn't know that he was actually Billy the Kid," Morrison said to her, and in her small, timid voice, she answered: "No, I didn't. He never did tell me. But I suspicioned it, though."

"But he told you when he came back from Santa Fe?"

"Yes, he told me then. And one day we was there a-talkin' and I wrote you a letter and he said, 'my half-brother,' and I said, 'Now Bill,' I says, 'now you know good and well it ain't,' and I says, 'now don't, don't story to me,' I says. 'I know you're Billy the Kid.' And he looked at me and laughed and he said, 'No, that's my half-brother.' I says, 'Well, now I can read between lines, I know you're Billy the Kid.' I says, 'That's all right if you are. It don't make me any difference. . .''

"And I says, "No, I ain't quittin' you. I'll live with you until you die or until I die." I said, "I'll never quit you as long as I live. I love you with all my heart." And he cried and grabbed me around the neck, and he says, "love you too, honey." And so he got all right—got over it."

CHAPTER TEN

IN BLACK AND WHITE

IN 1881, Billy the Kid was condemned to hang by the neck until he was dead. In 1949 —supposing he were still alive—he was still under sentence.

As Billy Roberts' representative, Morrison had some strenuous investigating to do before he could risk announcing his client as Billy the Kid. First he had to show that Billy the Kid was legally dead in order to have the death certificate set aside. Then he needed to assemble certified copies of all the indictments and other documents bearing on Billy's conviction so that proper steps might be taken to remove him from jeopardy.

It was a big job. For two years Morrison traveled, took notes, collected affidavits, gathered certified copies of legal instruments, and conducted an ever-widening correspondence. He did it at his own expense, for Brushy Bill had no money, because he was convinced of the soundness of his contentions. Paying little attention to rumor, hearsay, and legend, he concentrated on what had been set down in black and white regarding the windup of the Kid's career.

As the process went on, he found more and more indication that Billy the Kid's story had not been well and truly told. There were confusions, ambiguities, and out-and-out lies to be cleared up. He came to the conclusion that Billy was not always as bad as he had been represented to be, that, in some cases, he was more sinned against than sinning, and that he had grounds for asking that the noose be taken from around his neck.

He found that the very beginning of the Kid's career as a killer had, in all probability, been misrepresented. Old residents of Silver City have declared again and again that the story of his first murder—in defense of his "mother's" honor—is fictitious. They agree that he left home because he was put in jail for petty theft."

Likewise a number of the black marks chalked up against Billy in Lincoln County were not deserved. The killing of Buckshot Roberts at Blazer's Mill, on April 4, 1878, was one such case. Pat Garrett credits Billy with giving Buckshot a "mortal wound," and he was actually under federal indictment for this crime when he went on trial at Mesilla in 1881. He was not acquitted, however, as Garrett says. The indictment was thrown out of court.

The death of Joe Bernstein, clerk at the Mescalero Indian Agency, also was wrongfully laid at Billy's door. Pat Garrett and others say that Billy fired the shot which killed him, but later historians, including Garrett's editor, place the blame elsewhere.

Jim Carlyle's demise presents another case in which Billy's guilt is more than doubtful. The Authentic Life merely states that the volley which killed Carlyle when he crashed through Greathouse's window came from "within the house." Walter Noble Burns goes all the way and says that Billy "sent a bullet through him."   Billy's letter to the governor protesting that the posse surrounding the house was responsible for Carlyle's death has already been noted. It should be added that Morrison found no record in the courts of New Mexico charging Billy the Kid with this crime.

What happened to Billy after the law finally caught up with him needs also to be re-examined—and the records are there to show that he got something less than justice.

He went on trial for his life on April 8, 1881, in the old adobe building on the southeast corner of the plaza at Mesilla, considering himself the victim of a frame-up. He was firmly convinced, in the first place, that he had been deserted, without adequate cause, by Governor Wallace. He had made a bargains and had lived up to it, as he thought, to the letter—had submitted to nominal arrest, had testified at two trials, and had declared himself ready, in April, 1879, to answer at Lincoln for the murder of Sheriff Brady.

But then the deal began to come queer. District Attorney W. L. Rynerson had introduced a motion for change of venue to Dona Ana County. Billy, thinking he was being railroaded (as he probably was), had walked out of the jail and gone about his business. The business happened to be stealing livestock, and the law eventually caught up with him. He was taken first to Santa Fe and then to Mesilla to stand trial under the original indictment for the killing of Brady. This was the charge which Governor Wallace had urged him to face—and for which he had promised Billy a pardon in case things went wrong. Governor Wallace might have argued that since Billy had walked away from the Lincoln Jail, the agreement had been nullified. Billy's answer would have been that the original agreement did not include trail anywhere outside Lincoln County, and he had not left the game until he found that the rules were being changed.

At any rate, his first grievance was against the court and its officials, all of whom were more or less under the thumb of the Santa Fe Ring-the unsavory rulers of New Mexico. Judge Warren Bristol and District Attorney Rynerson had been friendly with the Murphy faction in the Lincoln troubles, and were, therefore, on good terms with the Ring. Both had been political opponents of Governor Wallace and friends of Governor Axtell, deposed by President Hayes.

The newspapers were against Billy too. The power of the Ring extended throughout the territory, and made itself felt in the editorial comments of many of the country weeklies.

S. H. Newman, editor of the Las Cruces Semi-Weekly, commented before the trial began: "We expect every day to hear of the Kid's escape. He is a notoriously dangerous character, has on several occasions escaped justice where escape appeared even more improbable than now, and has made his brag that he only wants to get free in order to kill three men— one of them being Governor Wallace. Should he break jail now, there is no doubt that he would immediately proceed to execute his threat."

Billy was quoted as saying, in regard to this statement: "Newman gave me a rough deal; has created prejudice against me, and is trying to incite a mob to lynch me. He sent me a paper which shows it. I think it a dirty, mean advantage to take of me, considering my situation and knowing I could not defend myself by word or act. But I suppose he thought he would give me a kick downhill."

The trial itself gave Billy his most profound grievance. He thought it was rigged from start to finish. After he had entered a plea of not guilty to the charge of killing Brady, the first witnesses were called. They included his bitterest enemies—such men as J. B. Matthews, J. J. Dolan, Bonny (for Bonifacio) Baca, George W. Peppin, and Bob Olinger. His friends, whose testimony might have cleared him, could not be located. Among these were Henry Brown, Robert McCormick, Ike Stockton, and Robert Widenmann. Widenmann in particular should have been there, for he was behind the adobe wall with Billy when Brady was shot, though he took no part in the action. Billy thought the authorities had made no real effort to pick up witnesses for the defense.

Only circumstantial evidence was introduced. None of the witnesses testified that the Kid had shot at Brady, or had hit Brady. All that was definitely established was the fact that four men had walked down the street in Lincoln on the morning of April 1, 1878— that two of them, both officers of the law, had been killed by shots fired by several men (exact number unknown) concealed behind an adobe wall near Tunstall's store—that the shooting had been done through holes in the aforementioned wall so that no one on the other side could identify positively the person or persons who fired the fatal shots—and that several men had appeared from behind the wall after the shooting was over.

It appeared furthermore that, although three men had been indicted for the murder, only one had been apprehended and that little if any effort had been made to catch the others.

The evidence, such as it was, being all in, the judge gave his charge to the jury. He instructed them to bring in a verdict of murder in the first degree or to declare the prisoner not guilty.

He then continued: "In this case in order to justify you in finding this defendant guilty of murder in the first degree under the peculiar circumstances as presented by the indictment and the evidence you should be satisfied and believe from the evidence to the exclusion of every reasonable doubt of the truth of several propositions:

1st That the defendant either inflicted one or more of the fatal wounds causing Brady's death or that he was present at the time and place of the killing and encouraged—incited—aided in—abetted-¬advised or commanded such killing.

2nd That such killing was without justification or excuse.

3rd That such killing of Brady was caused by inflicting upon his body a fatal gunshot wound.

And 4th That such fatal wound was either inflicted by the defendant from a premeditated design to effect Brady's death or that he was present at the time and place of the killing of Brady and from a premeditated design to effect his death he then and there encouraged —incited—aided in—abetted—advised or commanded such killing.

If he was so present—encouraging—inciting—aiding in—abetting-advising or commanding the killing of Brady he is as guilty as though he fired the fatal shot."

Billy thought this was carrying things pretty far, considering the fact that none of the witnesses had seen him do the thing he was charged with, whatever it was, exactly, and whatever the "peculiar circumstances" mentioned by the judge might have been (the indictment is missing from the file).

He expressed his views to a reporter for the Mesilla News who interviewed him after sentence was passed and asked if he expected the governor to pardon him:

Considering the active part Wallace took on our side and the friendly relations that existed between him and me, I think he ought to pardon me. Don't know that he will do it. When I was arrested for that murder, he let me out and gave me the freedom of the town and let me go about with my arms. When I got ready to go, I left. Think it hard that I should be the only one to suffer the extreme penalties of the law.

After the trial came the death sentence, the long ride back to Lincoln, the killing of Bell and Olinger, and the famous escape. Pat Garrett surrendered the now useless death warrant to the Secretary of State, at Santa Fe, on June 3, 1881, and no subsequent warrant was issued, so that Pat had no papers for the apprehension of the Kid on the night of July 14, 1881, when scene was played at Fort Sumner, though, of course, as an officer he had the right to pick up a condemned criminal anywhere he found him.

And this brings us to what can be found in black and white about the events which followed the shooting in Pete Maxwell's house. At once we encounter a most peculiar fact: THERE IS NO ACTUAL LEGAL PROOF OF THE DEATH OF BILLY THE KID.

A coroner's jury assembled and made a report—in fact two coroner's juries assembled and reported. But neither of these bodies made the proceedings a matter of official record. It will be said that the keeping of legal records in those days was notoriously lax—and anyone who knows even a little about such matters will agree. But records were being kept in San Miguel County at this time. A legally constituted justice of the peace presided over the inquest and should have made an entry in his books. He made no such entry.

And that was not all. Garrett was sheriff of Lincoln County and had stepped out of his own bailiwick when he entered San Miguel County. It was his duty to turn over an apprehended criminal to the sheriff of that county, whose name was Hilario Romero. Apparently he did not take the matter up with Romero, either before or after the killing, but went ahead and ran his own show.

Undoubtedly he had good reason for proceeding as he did.

There was a smoldering feud between Garrett and his men on the one hand and Romero and his men on the other. Romero had ignored Pat on one occasion when he wished to turn over some prisoners, and then, belatedly, had sent a posse which tried to take Deputy Barney Mason along to jail. Pat had won a pistol fight with a member of the gang and had refused to let one of the Romeros arrest him. Under these circumstances, there was not much point in asking for co-operation from the officers of the law in San Miguel County.

But irregular as Sheriff Garrett's proceedings may have been up to this point, they were impeccable compared to what followed. Mr. A. P. Anaya, former member of the legislature, now dead, described the inquest, or inquests, to George Fitzpatrick, editor of the New Mexico Magazine. "Mr. Anaya told me that he and a friend were called as members of the coroner's jury the night the Kid was killed," writes Mr. Fitzpatrick, "and that this jury wrote out a verdict stating simply that the Kid had come to his death as result of a wound from a gun in the hands of Pat Garrett, officer. Anaya claimed that this verdict was lost and that Garrett had Manuel Abreu write a more flowery one for filing. New signatures other than Anaya's and his friends' appear on the semi-official verdict. Anaya claimed Milnor Rudulph, who signed as 'presidente' of the jury, was not a member of the original jury which viewed the body.

Anaya wrote Fitzpatrick on April 2, 1936:

"*Yo he dicho tocante al Ditamen del Jurado Coronario que el ditamen que el Mismo Patt. escrivio y nosotros lo Firmamos no esta en Regis¬tro. el Patt Perdio ese papel y Luego Don Manuel Abreu le escribio uno en espanol. en Donde Puso al Mine Rudolfo Presidente, eso yo he dicho que no es verdad y pruevo eso.*"

Again on February 5, 1936, he wrote in English:

". . . there has been many things said in the other stories that are nothing but falsehoods, there are many things said that are just like the report that Pat Garret gave the court, he lost the report that we the coroner jury gave him and he got Mr. Manuel Abreu to write him another one. . . ."

What happened to the second purported death certificate? Garrett stated in his report to the governor that he filed it with the district attorney of the first judicial district. This should have meant that it was deposited in Las Vegas, the county seat of San Miguel County; but no such document could be found there. Records of this kind turn up in odd places, however, and one could not say the certificate had disappeared without checking every likely or unlikely place.

In handling Brushy Bill Roberts' case, Morrison had to find that death certificate if it was still in existence. Without some record that would stand up in a court of law, his man was not legally dead. If he could not be proved to be legally dead, there was no point in going to court to have the death record set aside, and proceedings would have to be taken up at some other point.

Morrison made diligent search, in person and by letter. He could find no evidence that Billy the Kid's death had ever been legally recorded anywhere in New Mexico.

In any event, as soon as might well be after the coroner's jury had acted, Garrett's attorney, Charles W. Green, applied for the governor's reward. He submitted a copy, plainly labeled as such, of the paper signed by Milnor Rudolph and his jurymen. This copy, together with the application for the reward money, was filed in the office of the secretary of the territory on July 20, 1881. Then another curious thing happened. Acting Governor W. G. Ritch would not validate Garrett's claim and refused to approve payment. As a result, Pat Garrett never collected the $500 offered by Governor Wallace for the apprehension of the Kid.

Ritch's ostensible reason for turning down Pat's application was strange and wonderful also. He interpreted Governor Wallace's offer as an unofficial and private act, and issued a statement which concluded: "In addition we will add as a fact that there was no record whatever, either in this office or at the Secretary's office of there having been a reward offered as set forth by the Attorney General, nor was there any record on file in said offices of a corresponding reward in any form."

This is truly amazing. For Acting Governor Ritch was secretary of state at the time Governor Wallace offered his reward, and he recorded Wallace's offer over his own signature in the same book which contains Garrett's letter of application. The entry begins:

NOW THEREFORE, I, Lewis Wallace, Governor of the Territory; by virtue of the power and authority vested in me by law and believing the end of justice will be best served thereby, do hereby offer a reward of five hundred dollars ($500.00) for the apprehension and arrest of said William Bonney, alias "Kid" and for his delivery to the Sheriff of Lincoln County at the County Seat of said county.

The proclamation is signed "Lewis Wallace, Governor. By the Governor. [Signed] W. G. Ritch."

Why did Ritch side-step payment of the reward by asserting the absence of a record which he had made himself? At this late date the question can probably be answered only by conjecture. The newspaper notices of the governor's offer, one of which Garrett referred to in his application, were not in proper legal form and could have been interpreted as extra-official on Wallace's part; but it was simply not true that there was no record of "a corresponding reward in any form."

One possible explanation would be Ritch's knowledge of the shaky character of the purported death certificate—a document which cannot now be, and perhaps never could have been, produced. It is conceivable also that the solution lies somewhere among the murky undercurrents of territorial politics.

And with that thought we are back with the Santa Fe Ring again. Charles W. Greene, Garrett's lawyer, was editor of the Santa Fe New Mexican and an important Ring man. Ritch, of course, was a friend of Governor Wallace and in opposition to the Ring. For some reason, Wallace's wing of the state government, including Ritch and the attorney general (who advised against paying the reward), did not want Garrett to get his money. The members of the Ring, all of whom had been Murphy-Dolan sympathizers and opposed to McSween and Billy the Kid, were, naturally, on the other side of the fence. That may explain, at least partly, why Charles W. Greene asked the legislature to do what Ritch would not or could not do. A bill was introduced to afford Garrett "relief." On the list of committeemen charged with considering this bill appears the name of W. T. Thornton, law partner of T. B. Catron—and T. B. Catron was the Big Man of the Santa Fe Ring. The legislature, of course, was heavily loaded with Ring supporters and henchmen. It was no trouble to get an act passed giving Garrett the money the governor had promised to pay.

It is interesting to note that the act credits Garrett with killing William Bonney "on or about the month of August, 1881," which adds to the complications by disposing of Billy a month later than the date given in the purported coroner's verdict. None of the gentlemen involved had any notion that their acts would be scrutinized so carefully almost seventy years later, or that a man named Brushy Bill Roberts would be frustrated by their lack of care and method.

All this confusion added up, in Morrison's view, to a series of doubts—doubts about Billy's guilt; doubts about the justice of his sentence; doubts about the governor's right to withhold a pardon; doubts about the actual circumstances of Billy's death and burial. The only way to get it all cleared up was to go to law about it. A pardon from the governor was to be the first step. After that the man who said he was Billy the Kid hoped to have his day in court in order that his representatives could produce whatever was down in black and white for or against him. It all came to nothing, for Brushy Bill Roberts was called to appear before a tribunal much higher than the courts of New Mexico.

EPILOGUE

WHEN A man comes back from the dead, he runs into a good many difficulties. First he has to have a convincing reason for wanting to come back. The living seem to have a strong prejudice against this sort of thing. It is inconsiderate, to say the least, for a dead man to thrust his problems upon people who already have enough to worry about. His friends are upset; his enemies are resentful; and the historians run a temperature.

Then comes the question: "Why, if you were so anxious to be alive, didn't you come back before?" After all, these resurrections are rare and rather fearful things. Only the most powerful impulse could induce a dead man to shake off the strong fetters of the grave; and if he felt such an impulse, he would hardly wait seventy years before doing something about it. It is quite natural to assume, therefore, that anyone who claims to be a character supposedly long since laid away must be an impostor. It is illogical to assume anything else.

Finally the candidate for revival has to convince the living that he is worthy to reassume his place among them. He finds that the evil he did has lived after him, and in some cases has grown and multiplied. The minute he steps across the threshold into the house of breath, the clamor begins: "Make him pay for all the crimes he was ever accused of!" In the case of a man who was under death sentence at the time he retired into the other world, the hangman is likely to be the first to welcome him back.

It seems to be a very troublesome business, all things considered, and probably the few who have been restored to the flesh would agree that the results hardly justify the effort.

When Brushy Bill Roberts decided to make his claim, he was immediately confronted by all these difficulties. Not many people took him seriously—first, because there seemed to be no good reason for his doing what he did. He explained his motives as best he could, saying that he wanted to correct some of the lies that had been told, stop running away, and die a free man. Still it was hard for those who knew about his case to understand anyone so near the end should wish to shatter the peace of his last days. In his place, wouldn't we have left well enough alone?

And, in the second place, if his claim was valid, why did he wait till he was ninety-one years old before making it? He explained that, too, by telling of at least one time when he thought of coming out of hiding. Even so, he hardly gave a satisfactory answer to the question, "Why did you wait so long?"

It is easier to deal with facts than with motives, of course. Consequently Bill Roberts sounds most impressive when he talks about the people he knew in his other life and the experiences they went through together. Furthermore he could cite the records to support some of his stories, and had affidavits sworn out by his old friends in order to establish his identity. The most important of these documents are reproduced at the end of this book and will have to stand on their merits. In the last analysis, the validity of the old man's claim depends on the reliability of the men and women who said they knew him, and on the credibility of the story he told.

As for the demand that he be punished for past crimes in case he was really Billy the Kid, that cry was, that cry was immediately raised when he asked the governor of New Mexico for a pardon. The hangman was still waiting after almost seventy years.

Perhaps luckily for him, there was in existence an impressive body of testimony which said he could not possibly be Billy Bonney. Many of the Kid's old companeros had asserted, at one time or another, that they knew for certain their friend was dead and buried. Pat Garrett told how it happened, and stuck to his story.

John W. Poe, who was with Garrett at the time Billy supposedly was shot, put his version in writing and John W. Poe was an honest man. The late Colonel Maurice Garland Fulton, who devoted half a lifetime to Lincoln County history, took no stock in Brushy Bill's story, as much as he knew of it.

To believe it at all, one has to assume that there was a conspiracy at Fort Sumner that July night in 1881—a conspiracy participated in by a good many people, including Pat Garrett. John W. Poe need not have been in on it, for he admits in his little book The Death of Billy the Kid that he had never seen the victim until a few seconds before the shooting. One has to believe also that the conspiracy was concealed year after year by the people involved, a hard theory for most people to swallow. Surely someone would have talked, sooner or later.

Without being too dogmatic about it, one might point out that the conspiracy theory is not completely impossible. The key people in Fort Sumner were friends of the Kid and might have kept their mouths shut. There is plenty of evidence that the community was on his side, almost to a man. John Poe himself says, "If the object of my visit had become known, I should have stood no chance for my life whatever."

It is true also that there was plenty of leakage of information about the conspiracy, if there was one. From the moment of Billy the Kid's death and burial, people were constantly saying that it was a put-up job. In fact there was so much talk that the story of Billy's escape actually loses probability through the multiplicity of theories about how it took place.

As for the possibility of keeping a notorious fact of this nature under cover for many years, we have only to look at the famous Fountain case for proof that it can be done. Colonel Fountain (who was one of Billy the Kid's lawyers in his trial at Mesilla) later became involved in a cattle feud and disappeared with his eight-year-old son, Henry, in 1896, near the White Sands. Three men were brought to trial, defended by Albert B. Fall, and acquitted on the grounds that the bodies of the supposedly murdered individuals could not be produced. To this day it is impossible to learn who killed Colonel Fountain, though a good many people have been involved in planning and carrying out the "murder". Men, and perhaps women, are undoubtedly still alive who know what happened, but they aren't talking.

If the fact of a conspiracy should be admitted, it is still hard to account for the motives of some of the men involved—especially Pat Garrett. The old stories often said that he and Billy worked it out together, but that seems unlikely. Neither Pat nor Billy were that kind of people. There is a possibility that Garrett might have been fooled by the resemblance between Billy and his "partner," but that seems unlikely too. Pat and Billy had known each other too long. It has been said that Pat went along with the scheme in order to collect the reward money—but the reward was small, and the expense of collecting it must have reduced it still further. The trick would not have paid off, even if Garrett had been the kind of person to play it—which he was not.

The only likely possibility left brings us back to the Santa Fe Ring, which handled Pat's claim for the reward money and saw to it that he was "relieved." If there is anything to Brushy Bill's story, Pat must have been a victim of circumstances somehow.

Without a doubt Billy the Kid was the hottest political potato in New Mexico. There were those who wanted him alive; there were those who wanted him dead; there were those who just wished he would go away. Perhaps Garrett, in imminent danger of mob violence, went along with a fiction which allowed Billy to get away and start a new life. Perhaps later on he was encouraged to stick to his story by politicians who were glad to be rid of the inconvenient young outlaw at any cost. If Brushy Bill's story is true, Pat must have become enmeshed somehow in these or similar intrigues and felt that his hands were tied.

In the midst of all these pros and cons, the original fact remains unaltered. Brushy Bill knew too much to have been an outsider.

He was not a literate man and could never have read up on his subject. His recollections are too detailed and precise to have come from oral sources. He must have been there, in the flesh, when these things happened.

And that brings up the final question—if Brushy Bill Roberts wasn't Billy the Kid, then who was he?

APPENDICES

The following pages contain transcripts of legal documents, letters, and other papers bearing on the career of Billy the Kid in New Mexico. They establish many pertinent facts about what actually happened at the end of Billy's career as an outlaw.

To show what may be deduced from these records, take the application for change of venue (Appendix B). District Attorney Rynerson filed the motion—not Billy himself, as is sometimes stated. It is not improbable, therefore, that Billy walked out of the Lincoln jail because he thought he was being railroaded, just as Brushy Bill Roberts said.

GOVERNOR WALLACE'S PROCLAMATION OF AMNESTY

15 November, 1878
Proclamation of Amnesty for Lincoln County Disorders
356
Proclamation by the Governor

For the information of the people of the United States, and of the citizens of the Territory of New Mexico in Especial, the undersigned announces that the disorders lately prevalent in Lincoln County in said Territory have been happily brought to an end. Persons having business and property interests therein, and who are themselves peaceably disposed, may go to and from that County without hindrance or molestation. Individuals resident there, but who have been driven away or who from choice sought safety elsewhere, are invited to return, under assurance that ample measures have been taken and are now and will be continued in force, to make them secure in person and property.

And that the people of Lincoln County may be helped more speedily to the management of their own affairs, as contemplated by law, and induce them to lay aside forever the divisions and feuds which by National Notoriety, have been so prejudicial to their locality and the whole Territory, the undersigned by virtue of authority in him vested, further proclaims a general Pardon for misdemeanors and offenses committed in the said County of Lincoln against the laws of the said Territory, in connection with the aforesaid disorders, between the first day of February, Eighteen hundred and Seventy Eight and the date of this Proclamation.

And it is expressly understood that the foregoing Pardon is upon the conditions and limitations following: It shall not apply except to officers of the United States Army stationed in the said County during the said disorders, and to persons who, at the time of commission of the offense or misdemeanor of which they may be accused, were with good intent, resident citizens of the said Territory, and who love hereafter kept the peace and conducted themselves in all respects as become good citizens. Neither shall it be pleaded by any bar of conviction under indictment now found or returned for any such crimes or misdemeanors, nor operate the release of any party undergoing pains and penalties consequent upon sentence heretofore had for any crime or misdemeanor.

In Witness Whereof I have hereunto set my hand and caused the Seal of the Territory of New Mexico to be affixed.

[Seal]

Done at the City of Santa Fe this the thirteenth day of November A. D. Eighteen hundred and Seventy-Eight.

By the Governor
W. G. RITCH, *Secretary*

LEWIS WALLACE
Governor of New Mexico

Entered of record November 15th A. D. 1878
W. G. RITCH, *Secretary*

(Copy certified by Alicia Romero, Secretary of State, Aug. 21, 1950)

Appendix B

The Change of Venue

APPENDIX B:1

RYNERSON'S MOTION

The District Court of the Third Judicial District of County of
Lincoln, Territory of New Mexico, at the April A.D. 1879 Term Thereof
Cause No. 244 - Murder
(532. Dona Ana County.)
The Territory of New Mexico
vs
John Middleton
Henry Brown and
William Bonny alias Kid
alias William Antrim

Now comes the said Territory by her attorney W. L. Rynerson, District Attorney of the said Third Judicial District and moves the Court to change the Venue in the above entitled Cause as to the said defendant William Bonny alias "Kid" alias William Antrim for reasons set forth in the following affidavit.

W. L. RYNERSON
District Attorney
Territory of New Mexico, County of Lincoln

W.L. Rynerson district attorney for the Third Judicial District of the said territory of New Mexico, being first duly sworn deposes and says that justice cannot be done the said Territory on the Trial of said defendant in the said County of Lincoln for the reason that jurors in attendance and liable to be summoned for the Trial of said defendant from partisanship in the troubles existing in the said county have so prejudiced the said Jurors that they cannot fairly and impartially try the said defendant and for the further reason that the said Jurors and witnesses in said Cause are so intimidated by lawless men in said Lincoln County, that the said Jurors and Witnesses cannot fearlessly perform their respective duties at said Trial in said Lincoln County.

W. L. RYNERSON

Sworn to and subscribed before me in open Court, April 21, A.D. 1879

Louis H. Baldy, *Clerk*

APPENDIX B:2

THE SUPPORTING AFFIDAVIT

Affidavit and Motion for Change of Venue
Cause 244-
(532. Dona Ana County)
Territory of New Mexico, County of Lincoln

Marion Turner and John Long being severally sworn depose and say severally that they have heard the foregoing affidavit read and heard the contents thereof and that the matters and things as therein stated are true.

JOHN LONG
MARION TURNER

Sworn and subscribed before me April 22, 1879

Louis H. Baldy, *Clerk*

APPENDIX B:3

CHANGE OF VENUE GRANTED

Eighth Day, Tuesday, April 22, 1879
Court met pursuant to adjournment
Present as of yesterday
243 - Murder

The Territory
VS
John Middleton
Henry Brown
William Bonny
Alias "Kid" Alias William Antrim

This Cause coming on to be heard upon the motion of the Plaintiff herein by W. L. Rynerson Esq District Attorney therefor, for a change of venue in Said Court as to said Defendant William Bonny-alias Kid, alias William Antrim, for reasons set forth in the affidavit attached to Said motion now on file herein, and the motion being submitted to the Court and the Court being fully advised in the premises, sustains Said motion Said Defendant being present with his counsel to which ruling of the Court the Defendant excepts.

It is therefore ordered by the Court that the venue in this Cause, as to the Defendant William Bonny alias "Kid" alias William Antrim herein, be and the same hereby is changed to the County of Dona Ana in the Third Judicial District, Territory of New Mexico, and it is further ordered that the Clerk of this Court make an exemplified copy of the proceedings had in this Cause in this Court and transmit the same together with the Original Papers in Said Cause to the District Court in and for the County of Dona Ana, Territory of New Mexico.

And now further comes the Said Territory by her said District Attorney and moves the Court that Isaac Ellis, B. F. Baca and Jacob B. Mathews who have been summoned to appear and testify as witnesses in Said Cause on the part of the Territory and are now present in Court be required to enter into their personal recognizance respectively to appear as such witnesses at the next Ensuing Term of the Court in and for Said County of Dona Ana, which said motion is sustained by the Court. It is therefore ordered that Said Witnesses be and they thereby are required to enter into their personal recognizance respectively in the sum of ($1,000.00) One Thousand Dollars for their appearance as aforesaid. And now comes the said Ellis, the said B. F. Baca and the said Jacob B. Mathews who in open Court each for himself does acknowledge that he is indebted to the Territory of New Mexico in the Penal Sum of One Thousand Dollars, for the payment of which well and truly to be made he binds Himself, his heirs, executors and administrators upon the condition ever that if he shall personally appear at the next ensuing Term of the District Court for the Third Judicial District of the Territory of New Mexico to be held in and for the County of Dona Ana as a witness on the part of the Territory in Said Cause and shall remain in attendance thereat from day to day and from Term to Term until discharged by Authority of law then this obligation to be void otherwise to remain in full force and effect.

244

Now comes the Plaintiff herein by her District Attorney W. L. Rynerson Esq. and the Defendant William Bonny, alias Kid alias William Antrim, herein appearing in his own proper person accompanied by his counsel. Whereupon the said Plaintiff by her said attorney moves the court, that the Venue in this Cause be changed as to the said Defendant William Bonny alias Kid alias William Antrim for the reasons set forth in the affidavit therefor filed herein and the Court being fully advised in the premises sustains Said motion.

It is therefore ordered that the Venue in this Cause as to the said Defendant William Bonny alias Kid alias William Antrim be and the same hereby is changed to the County of Dona Ana in the Third Judicial District of the Territory of New Mexico. And it is further ordered that the Clerk of this Court make an exemplified Copy of the proceedings had in this Cause in this Court and transmit the Same together with the original Papers in Said Cause to the District Court in and for the said County of Dona Ana to which ruling and order of this Court the Defendant Excepts.

Proceedings of the Eighth Day of the District Court of the Third Judicial District held in Lincoln, New Mexico on Tuesday April 22, 1879, and found of Record in Volume B on Pages 316-317-318 of the District Court Records of Lincoln County, New Mexico.

District Court Lincoln County, State of New Mexico, Carrizozo, 13th day of October A. D. 1949

J. G. MOORE, *Clerk*
[signed]
OTELA E. VEGA, *Deputy*

APPENDIX C

BILLY THE KID'S TRIAL

APPENDIX C:1

THE MISSING INDICTMENT

Geraldine S. Mathisen, District Court Clerk
Third Judicial District, Phone 11, Las Cruces, New Mexico October 19, 1949
To WHOM IT MAY CONCERN:

I, Geraldine S. Mathisen, Clerk of the District Court of the Third Judicial District of New Mexico do hereby certify that I have made a due and diligent search of the records here in this office, and fail to find the indictment in Criminal Cause No. 532 entitled Territory of New Mexico versus William Bonney alias "Kid" alias William Antrim

Dated at Las Cruces, New Mexico this the 19th day of October, A.D. 1949.

[s] GERALDINE S. MATHISEN
District Court Clerk of the Third Judicial District in and for the county of Dona Ana, State of New Mexico

APPENDIX C:2

REQUEST FOR INSTRUCTIONS BY DEFENDANT'S COUNSEL

In the District Court, Dona Ana County, N. M.
March 1881 Term
Cause 532
Territory of New Mexico
vs
William Bonny, alias Kid, alias William Antrim (Murder)

Instructions asked for by Defendants Counsel. The Court is asked to instruct the Jury as follows, to wit:

1st Instruction asked.

Under the evidence the Jury must either find the Defendant guilty of murder in the 1st degree, or acquit him.

2nd Instruction asked.

The Jury will not be justified in finding the Defendant guilty of murder in the 1st degree unless they are satisfied, from the evidence, to the exclusion of all reasonable doubt, that the defendant actually fired the shot that caused the death of the deceased Brady, and that such shot was fired by the Defendant with a premeditated design to effect the death of the deceased, or that the Defendant was present and actually assisted in firing the fatal shot or shots that caused the death of deceased, and that he was present and in a position to render such assistance from a premeditated design to effect the death of the deceased.

3rd Instruction asked.

If the Jury are satisfied from the evidence to the exclusion of all reasonable doubt that the Defendant was present at the time of the firing of the shot or shots that caused the death of the deceased Brady, yet, before they will be justified in finding the Defendant guilty, they must be further satisfied from the evidence and the evidence alone, to the exclusion of all reasonable doubt, that the Defendant either fired the shots that killed the deceased, or some of them, or that he assisted in firing said shot or shots, and that he fired said shot or shots or assisted in firing the same or assisted the parties who fired the same either by his advice, encouragement, or procurement or command from a premeditated design to effect the death of Brady. If the Jury entertains any reasonable doubt upon any of these points, they must find a verdict of acquittal.

A. J. FOUNTAIN
J. D. BAIL
Attorneys for Defendant

APPENDIX C:3

JUDGE BRISTOL'S INSTRUCTIONS TO THE JURY

Territory of New Mexico District Court
3rd Judicial District
Dona Ana County
April Term A. D. 1881
Murder- 1st Degree
The Territory of New Mexico
Vs
William Bonney alias Kid alias William Antrim

Gentlemen of the Jury: The defendant in this case William Bonney alias Kid alias William Antrim is charged in and by the indictment against him which has been laid before you with having committed in connection with certain other persons this crime of murder in the County of Lincoln in the 3rd Judicial District of the Territory of New Mexico in the month of April of the year 1878 by then and there unlawfully killing one William Brady by inflicting upon his body certain fatal gunshot wounds from a premeditated design to effect his death.

The case is here for trial by a change of venue from the said county of Lincoln.

The facts alleged in the indictment if true constitute murder in the 1st and highest degree and whether these allegations are true or not are, for, you to determine from the evidence which you have heard and which is now submitted to you for your careful consideration. In the matter of determining what your verdict shall be it will be improper for you to consider anything except the evidence before you as jurors are the exclusive judges or the weight of the evidence. You are the exclusive judges of the credibility of the witnesses. It is for you to determine whether the testimony of any witness whom you have heard is to be believed or not. You are also the exclusive judges whether the evidence is sufficiently clear and strong to satisfy your minds that the defendant is guilty.

There is no evidence tending to show that the killing of Brady was either justifiable or excusable in law—as a matter of law therefore such killing was unlawful and whoever committed the deed or was present and advised aided or abetted and consented to such killing committed the crime of murder in some one of the degrees of murder.

There is no evidence before you showing that the killing of Brady is murder in any other degree than the first—

Your verdict therefore should be either that the defendant is guilty of murder in the 1st degree or that he is not guilty at all under this indictment.

Murder in the 1st degree consists in the killing of one human being by another without authority of law and from a premeditated design to effect the death of the person killed—

Every killing of one human being by another that is not justifiable or excusable would be necessarily a killing without authority of law. As I have already instructed you to constitute murder in the 1st degree it is necessary that the killing should have been perpetrated from a premeditated design to effect the death of the person killed—

As to this premeditated design I charge you that to render a design to kill premeditated it is not necessary that such design to kill should exist in the mind for any considerable length of time before the killing.

If the design to kill is completely formed in the mind but for a moment before inflicting the fatal wound it would be premeditated and in law the effect would be the same as though the design to kill had existed for a long time—

In this case in order to justify you in finding this defendant guilty of murder in the 1st degree under the peculiar circumstances as presented by the indictment and the evidence you should be satisfied and believe from the evidence to the exclusion of every reasonable doubt of the truth of several propositions.

1st- That the defendant either inflicted one or more of the fatal wounds causing Brady's death or that he was present at the time and place of the killing and encouraged— incited—aided in—abetted—advised or commanded such killing—

2nd- That such killing was without justification or excuse

3rd- That such killing of Brady was caused by inflicting upon his body a fatal gunshot wound. And

4th- that such fatal wound was either inflicted by the defendant from a premeditated design to effect Brady's death or that he was present at the time and place of the killing of Brady and from a premeditated design to effect his death he then and there encouraged —incited—aided in—abetted—advised or commanded such killing_

If he was so present—encouraging—inciting—aiding in—abetting_ advising or commanding the killing of Brady, he is as much guilty as though he fired the fatal shot—

I have charged you that to justify you in finding the defendant guilty of murder in the 1st degree you should be satisfied from the evidence to the exclusion of every reasonable doubt that the defendant is actually guilty. As to what would be or would not be a reasonable doubt of guilt I charge you that belief in the guilt of the defendant to the exclusion of every reasonable doubt does not require you to so believe absolutely and to a mathematical certainty—That is to justify a verdict of guilty it is not necessary for you to be as certain that the defendant is guilty as you are that two and two are four or that two and three are five.

Merely a vague conjecture or bare probability that the defendant may be innocent is not sufficient to raise a reasonable doubt of his guilt. If all the evidence before you which you believe to be true convinces and directs your understanding and satisfies your reason and judgment while acting upon it conscientiously under your oath as jurors and if this evidence leaves in your minds an abiding conviction to a moral certainty that the defendant is guilty of the crime charged against him: then this would be proof of guilt to the exclusion of every reasonable doubt and would justify you in finding the defendant guilty—

You will apply the evidence to this case according to the instructions I have given you and determine whether the defendant is guilty of murder in the 1st degree or not guilty—

Murder in the 1st degree is the greatest crime known to our laws. The Legislature of this Territory has enacted a law prescribing that the punishment for murder in the 1st degree shall be death—

This then is the law: no other punishment than death can be imposed for murder in the 1st degree—

If you believe and are satisfied therefore from the evidence before you to the exclusion of every reasonable doubt that the defendant is guilty of murder in the 1st degree then it will be your duty to find a verdict that the defendant is guilty of murder in that degree naming murder in the 1st degree in your verdict and also saying in your that the defendant shall suffer the punishment of death— If from the evidence you do not believe to the exclusion of every reasonable doubt that the defendant is guilty of murder in the 1st degree or if you entertain a reasonable doubt as to the guilt of the defendant- then in that case your verdict should be not guilty.

No. 532

Territory vs William Bonny alias "Kid" alias William Antrim (Murder)

Charge to trial Jury
Filed in my office this 9th day of April A. D. 1881

[S] GEORGE R. BOWMAN
Clerk

APPENDIX C:4

THE JURY

Page 390 Eleventh Day, April 8th A D 1881—Cont'd

And now there being twelve qualified Petit Jurors present and both parties declaring themselves satisfied with the Jury as it now stands the following Jury is accepted to wit:

Refugio Bernal

Jesus Telles

Crecencio Bustillos

 Luis Sedillos

Felipe Lopez

Pedro Onopa

Merced Lucero

Pedro Serna

Jesus Silva

Pedro Martinez

Hilario Moreno

Benito Montoya

Twelve good and lawful men of the body of the Third Judicial District, duly drawn accepted *empanelled* and sworn to well and truly try and true deliverance make between the Territory of New Mexico and the prisoner at the bar and a true verdict give according to the evidence. And after hearing a part of the evidence the said Jury are placed in charge of two sworn officers until the opening of Court tomorrow.

Whereupon Court adjourned until tomorrow morning at 10 o'clock

[s] Warren Bristol
Judge

APPENDIX C:5

THE VERDICT

Page 391
Twelfth Day, April 9th A.D. 1881
Court met pursuant to adjournment.
Present as of yesterday
Territory of New Mexico
vs
William Bonny alias "Kid" alias William Antrim (Murder)

Now comes the Plaintiff herein by Simon B. Newcomb Esq. District Attorney therefore and the Defendant appearing in his own proper person and accompanied by John D. Bail Esq. and A.J. Fountain Esq. his attorneys and the jury empanelled yesterday in said cause being present and said Jury having heard all the evidence and the arguments of counsel and received the instructions of the Court, retire to deliberate, accompanied by two sworn officers. And after deliberation the said Jury return into Court and upon their oaths do say "We the Jury in the above entitled cause to find the Defendant guilty of murder in the first degree and do assess his punishment at death"

[s] Warren Bristol
Judge

APPENDIX C:6

THE SENTENCE

Page 406 Fifteenth Day, April 13th A D 1881—Continued
Territory of New Mexico
vs
William Bonny alias "Kid" alias William Antrim (murder)

Now comes the Plaintiff herein by Simon B., Newcomb Esq. District Attorney therefor and the Defendant appearing in his own proper person and accompanied by counsel and the Court being fully advised as to the sentence to be passed upon said Defendant in pursuance of the verdict rendered in said cause at a former day of this Term; and the Defendant being asked if he had anything to say why sentence should not be passed upon him in pursuance of said verdict says nothing.

It is therefore considered by the Court here that the said Defendant, William Bonny, alias Kid alias William Antrim be taken to the County of Lincoln in the Third Judicial District of the Territory of New Mexico by the Sheriff of said county of Lincoln and that he, the said William Bonny, alias Kid, alias William Antrim be confined in prison in said county of Lincoln, by the Sheriff of such county until on Friday the 13th day of May in the year of our Lord One Thousand Eight Hundred and eighty-one. That on the day aforesaid between the hours of nine of the clock in the forenoon and three of the clock in the afternoon he, the said William Bonny alias Kid alias William Antrim, be taken from such prison to some suitable and convenient place of execution within the said County of Lincoln, by the Sheriff of such county and that then and there, on that day and between the aforesaid hours thereof, by the Sheriff of said county of Lincoln, he, the said William Bonny, alias Kid, alias William Antrim be hanged by the neck until his body be dead.

Judgment and sentence herein was pronounced upon the said defendant at five o'clock and fifteen minutes in the afternoon of this 13th day of April A.D. 1881. Ordered by the Court that a certified record of the Judgment of the Court be transmitted to the Governor of the Territory without delay, which is accordingly done. Whereupon Court adjourned until tomorrow morning at 10 o'clock.

[s] Warren Bristol
Judge

APPENDIX C:7

THE DEATH WARRANT

Death Warrant of Billy the Kid
Ex. Rec. 506

To the Sheriff of Lincoln County, New Mexico, Greeting:

At the March term, A.D. 1881, of the District Court for the Third Judicial District of New Mexico, held at La Mesilla in the county of Dona Ana, William Bonney, alias Kid, alias William Antrim, was duly convicted of the crime of murder in the 1st Degree; and on the fifteenth day of said term, the same being the thirteenth day of April, A.D. 1881, the Judgment and Sentence of said Court were pronounced against the said William Bonney, alias Kid, alias William Antrim, upon said conviction according to law. Whereby the said William Bonney, alias Kid, alias William Antrim, was adjudged and sentenced to be hanged by the neck until dead, by the Sheriff of the said county of Lincoln, within said county.

Therefore, you, the Sheriff of the said county of Lincoln, are hereby commanded that on Friday, the Thirteenth day of May, A. D. 1881, Pursuant to the said Judgment and sentence of the said Court, you take the said William Bonney, alias Kid, alias William Antrim, from the county jail of the county of Lincoln where he is now confined, to some safe and convenient place within the said County, and there, between the hours of Ten O'clock, A. M., and three O'clock, P. M., of said day, you hang the said William Bonney, alias Kid, alias William Antrim by the neck until he is dead. And make due return of your acts hereunder.

[SEAL] Done at Santa Fe in the Territory of New Mexico, this 30th day of April, A. D. 1881.

Witness my hand and the great seal of the Territory.

[signed] LEW WALLACE
Governor New Mexico

By the governor
W. G. RITCH, Secretary, N. M.

APPENDIX C:8

THE SHERIFF'S RETURN OF THE DEATH WARRANT

Death Warrant
Territory
vs
Wm Bonney, alias Kid
Lincoln, Lincoln County, New Mexico May 24th 1881.

I hereby certify that the within Warrant was not served owing to the fact that the within named prisoner escaped before the day set for serving said Warrant.

PAT F. GARRETT, *Sheriff*
Lincoln County, New Mexico
2 Ex Rec 515

FILED. June 3, 1881
W. G. RITCH, *Sec.* N.M.

APPENDIX D

THE REPORT OF THE CORONER'S JURY

APPENDIX D:1

THE CORONER'S JURY
(TRANSLATION)

Report of the Coroner's Jury (translation of a photostat copy of a purported original
which was never filed in San Miguel County)
Territory of New Mexico Precinct No. 27
County of San Miguel

To the attorney of the First Judicial District of the Territory of New Mexico.

GREETING:
This 15th day of July, A. D. 1881, I, the undersigned, Justice of the Peace of the
Precinct above named, received information that there had been a death in Fort Sumner
in said Precinct and immediately on receiving the information I proceeded to the said
place and named Milnor Rudolph, Jose Silva, Antonio Saavedra, Pedro Antonio Lucero,
Lorenzo Jaramillo, and Sabal Gutierres a jury to investigate the matter, and, meeting in
the house of Lucien B. Maxwell, the said jury proceeded to a room in said house where
they found the body of William H. Bonney alias "Kid" with a bullet wound in the chest,
and, having examined the body, they examined the evidence of Pedro Maxwell, which
evidence is as follows: "As I was lying on my bed in my room about midnight on the
14th day of July,

Patrick F. Garrett entered my room and sat down on the edge of my bed to talk to
me. Soon after Garrett had seated himself William Bonney entered and approached my
bed with a pistol in his hand and asked me, 'Who is it? Who is it?' and then Patrick F.
Garrett fired two shots at him, the said William Bonney, and the said Bonney fell upon
one side of my fireplace, and I left the room. When I returned three or four minutes after
the shots, the said Bonney was dead."

The jury has found the following verdict: "We of the jury unanimously find that
William Bonney was killed by a shot in the left breast, in the region of the heart, fired
from a pistol in the hand of Patrick F. Garrett, and our verdict is that the act of the said
Garrett was justifiable homicide, and we are unanimous in the opinion that the gratitude

of the whole community is due to the said Garrett for his act and that he deserves to be rewarded."

M. RUDULPH
President

ANTON SABEDRA
PEDRO ANTO LUCERO
JOSE X SILBA
SABAL X GUTIERREZ
LORENZO X JARAMILLO

All of which information I bring to your notice.

ALEJANDRO SEGURA
Justice of the Peace

APPENDIX D:2

LETTER FROM THE DISTRICT ATTORNEY FOR THE FOURTH JUDICIAL DISTRICT

Jose E. Armijo, District Attorney
E. R. Cooper, Assistant
Counties: San Miguel, Mora and Guadalupe
Office of the District Attorney
Fourth Judicial District
State of New Mexico
Las Vegas, New Mexico
August 14, 1951

Mr. Wm. V. Morrison 1312 Arizona
El Paso, Texas

Dear Sir:

I wish to acknowledge receipt of your letter of August 9, 1951 requesting a certified copy of the coroner's verdict on the death of Wm. H. Bonney, alias Billy the Kid.

I am sorry I cannot comply with your request because of the fact that such a record is not now, and never has been, among the records of this office. I am sorry, also that I am at a loss to direct you to the office where you could obtain a copy of such record.

Such a verdict, if it existed, should have been filed in the office of the County Clerk. However, the original San Miguel County (Which at that time comprised what is now De Baca County) has been split up so many times that it is now but a small fraction of its original size. Perhaps such a record can be found in the office of the County Clerk of Guadalupe County, (County seat being Santa Rosa, New Mexico), or in the office of the County Clerk of De Baca County (county seat being Fort Sumner, New Mexico). Both these counties were formed out of what once was San Miguel County.

I am sorry the Attorney General's office misinformed you as to such record. I have never seen such record and it is my opinion that it would be almost an impossibility to locate such a record at this late date because of the poor condition and method of keeping records at the time Billy the Kid is purported to have been killed by Pat Garrett.

Again, I am sorry I cannot be of service to you in this matter, but I do wish you success in locating such record.

Very truly yours,
[s] Jose E. Armijo
District Attorney

APPENDIX D:3

LETTER FROM THE COUNTY CLERK OF DEBACA COUNTY

County Clerk and Ex-Officio Recorder
De Baca County

Fort Sumner, New Mexico
STATE OF NEW MEXICO –ss.
County of De Baca

I, Cecil W. Williams, County Clerk within and for the County of De Baca, State of New Mexico, Do Hereby Certify that I have searched the records in my office and I fail to find anything pertaining to the Coroner's Jury Verdict in the Case of "Billy the Kid."

Witness my hand and seal of said office this 21st day of August, 1951.

[SEAL]

[S] CECIL W. WILLIAMS

County Clerk

APPENDIX D:4

LETTER FROM THE COUNTY CLERK OF GUADALUPE COUNTY

Jose M. Maestas, Jr., Clerk of Guadalupe County
Santa Rosa, New Mexico
State of New Mexico –ss.
County of Guadalupe

I, Jose M. Maestas, Jr. County Clerk within and for the County of Guadalupe, State of New Mexico, do hereby certify that I have searched the records in my office and I fail to find anything pertaining to the Coroner's Jury Verdict in the Case of "Billy the Kid."

Witness my hand and seal of said office this 21st day of August,1951.

[SEAL]
[S] JOSE M. MAESTAS, JR. *County Clerk*

APPENDIX D:5

LETTER FROM THE DEPUTY DISTRICT CLERK OF THE FOURTH JUDICIAL DISTRICT

Office of the
Clerk of the District Court
Las Vegas, New Mexico

October 31, 1949

Mr. William V. Morrison
3120 Wheeling Street
El Paso, Texas.

Dear Mr. Morrison,

I sent your letter requesting the Coroner's Verdict of the purported death of William H. Bonney to the Clerk of the District Court of De Baca County, as there is no record in this office of any Coroner's Verdict, and we do not have the records of De Baca County in this office.

Very truly yours,

[s] CARMEN ARMIJO
Deputy District Court Clerk

APPENDIX D:6

LETTER FROM THE SECRETARY OF STATE FOR THE STATE OF NEW MEXICO

State of New Mexico
Department of State
Office of the Secretary of State
Santa Fe

November 21, 1949

Mr. William V. Morrison
3120 Wheeling Street
El Paso, Texas

Dear Mr. Morrison:

This will acknowledge receipt of your letter dated November 12th.

Our records failed to disclose the death record or Coroner's report with reference to the purported death of William H. Bonney, alias the Kid, alias William Antrim.
As requested, I am enclosing a certified copy of the Return on Death Warrant which was issued by the Sheriff of Lincoln County on May 24th, 1881.

Also enclosed is your Official Receipt in the amount of $3.00 in full payments of statements dated October 27th, and November 21st.

Yours very truly,

[s] ALICIA ROMERO
(Mrs. M. A. Romero) Secretary of State

APPENDIX E

THE REWARD

APPENDIX E:1

GOVERNOR WALLACE'S OFFICIAL OFFER

REWARD Territory of New Mexico
vs
William Bonney alias "The Kid", A Fugitive
[Indictment in Lincoln County District Court for Murder]
Executive Office
Territory of New Mexico

WHEREAS William Bonney, alias "the Kid" stands charged under indictment issued from the District Court in and for the County of Lincoln, of the crime of murder committed in said county; and

WHEREAS, the said William Bonney alias "The Kid" is a fugitive from justice

Now THEREFORE, I, Lewis Wallace, Governor of the Territory; by virtue of the power and authority vested in me by the law and believing the end of justice will best be served thereby, do hereby offer a reward of five hundred dollars ($500.00) for the apprehension and arrest of said William Bonney alias "The Kid" and for his delivery to the Sheriff of Lincoln County at the County seat of said county.

In witness whereof I have hereunto set my hand and have caused the Great Seal of the Territory to be hereto affixed this 13th day of December, 1880.

[S] LEW WALLACE
Governor
[ORIGINAL SEAL]

By the Governor
[s] W. G. Raul
Secretary of New Mexico

(Copy certified by Beatrice B. Roach, Secretary of State, August 23, 1951)

APPENDIX E:2

GOVERNOR RITCH'S REFUSAL TO APPROVE GARRETT'S APPLICATION

July 21

In the matter of the application by Patrick F. Garrett for a reward claimed to have been offered May 1881 for the capture of Wm Bonny alias the Kid

[Action on Petition Suspended]
Executive Department
Territory of New Mexico

July 21, 1881

July 20th 1881 Pat. F. Garrett, Sheriff of Lincoln County, appeared and presented a bill for $500. claiming it as a reward offered on or about the 7th of May 1881 by the late Governor, Lew Wallace, for the capture of said Bonny.

As evidence of said offer having been made the affidavit of publication thereof made by Chas. W. Green, the editor and manager of the Daily New Mexican, was presented with said bill, as also was presented a statement of the proceedings and verdict of a coroner's jury at Ft. Sumner in San Miguel County upon the body of said Bonny, captured as aforesaid, and a statement of Garrett directed to this office of his doings in the premises.

Upon examination of said papers it was deemed important that the opinion of the Attorney General be taken thereon and they were at once transmitted to that office. On the following day, the papers with the opinion of Hon. Wm. Breeden Attorney General were filed.

Said opinion is quite full. We quote the closing paragraphs as sufficient in this connection, to wit:

BILLY THE KID

$500 REWARD

"I will pay five hundred dollars reward to any person or persons, will capture William Bonny, alias the Kid, and deliver him to any Sheriff of New Mexico, satisfactory proof of identity will be required."

[S] LEW WALLACE
Governor of New Mexico"

"This certainly appears to be the personal offer of Governor Wallace, and it seems he did nothing to indicate that it was intended as an executive act, on behalf of, and to bind the Territory.

"If the reward should be paid, it is very probable, that the Legislature would approve the payment if so desired, and that no objection would be raised, or that it will provide for its payment, if it remains unpaid, at the next session thereof; but if the Governor should now direct the payment of the claim, he would doubtless expose himself to the charge of misappropriation of the Territorial funds, in case the Legislature should refuse to ratify and approve the payment." In addition, we will add as a fact that there was no record whatever, either in this office or at the Secretary's office of there having been a reward offered as set forth by Attorney General, nor was there any record on file in said offices of a corresponding reward in any form.

The opinion of the Attorney General appearing to be consistent with the law and the facts, decision is rendered accordingly and the Governor declines to allow the reward at this time. Believing how- ever, that Mr. Garrett, has an equitable claim against the Territory for said reward; further action at this office will simply be suspended until the case can be properly represented to the next Legislature Assembly.

[s] W. G. RITCH
Acting Governor New Mexico

APPENDIX E:3

THE LEGISLATIVE ACT

1882—Private Laws of New Mexico-25th Session
Relief of Pat Garrett—Chapter 101 page 191
Chapter C1
AN ACT for the Relief of Pat Garrett.

Contents

Section 1. Authorizes the payment of $500 reward for the arrest of the "Kid."

WHEREAS, The Governor of New Mexico did, on or about the 7th day of May, A. D., 1881, issue his certain proclamation in words and figures as follows, to-wit:

"I will pay five hundred dollars reward to any person or persons who will capture William Bonney, alias 'The Kid', and deliver him to any Sheriff of New Mexico. Satisfactory proof of identity will be required."

[Signed] LEW WALLACE,
Governor of New Mexico

AND WHEREAS, Pat Garrett was at that time Sheriff of Lincoln County, and did, on or about the month of August, 1881, in pursuance of the above reward and by virtue of a warrant placed in his hands for that purpose, attempted to arrest said William Bonney, and in said attempt did kill said William Bonney at Fort Sumner, in the County of San Miguel, in the Territory of New Mexico, and wherefore, said Garrett is justly entitled to the above reward, and payment thereof has been refused upon a technicality.

Be it enacted by the Legislative Assembly of the Territory of New Mexico:

Section I. The Territorial Auditor is hereby authorized to draw a warrant upon the Territorial Treasurer of the Territory of New in favor of Pat Garrett for the sum of five hundred dollars, we out of any funds in the Territorial treasury not otherwise especially appropriated, in payment of the reward of five hundred dollars heretofore offered by his Excellency, Governor Lew Wallace, for the arrest of William Bonney, alias "The Kid."

Section 2. This act shall take effect and be in force from and after its passage.

Approved February 18, 1882.

AFFIDAVITS

1. Severo Gallegos

2. Martile Able

3. Jose B. Montoya

4. Dewitt Travis

5. Robert E. Lee

APPENDIX F:1

AFFIDAVIT OF SEVERO GALLEGOS

STATE OF NEW MEXICO -ss.
County of Lincoln

Before me, the undersigned authority, on this day, personally appeared Mr. Severo Gallegos of Lincoln County, New Mexico, who, upon his oath, deposes and says:

That his name is Severn Gallegos, that he is past 82 years of age, that he is a son of Lucas Gallegos, deceased; that he is a half-brother of Florencio Chavez, who fought in the Lincoln County War, and rode with Wm. Bonney, known as Billy the Kid.

This affiant further states that Billy the Kid many times visited in the Gallegos Home; that he stayed there some times over night and that he ate many meals there; that the Kid and Florencio Chavez did much target practice at their home in San Patricio; that Billy was quick on the draw; that he fired a rifle left handed and six shooters with both hands; that he would shoot from the hip and that he was known to be a good shot.

This affiant further states that Billy the Kid was a small man when he was young; that he had small feet and hands with large wrists; that he had two large teeth in the front of his mouth; that he had blue-grey eyes with small brown spots in them; that his nose was straight, high cheek bones and large ears; that he had dark hair; that he stood as straight as a whip, and rode a horse straight in the saddle.

This affiant further states that he made many visits to see Billy the Kid in the Lincoln Jail; that he took berries to the jail for Billy to eat; that he saw Billy escape from the Jail in April, 1881; that he never saw Billy the Kid again until the first day of April, 1950; that after talking to Billy for several hours on April first, this affiant knows from conversation and looking him over, that Billy the Kid was the same person as O.L. Roberts who visited here in Ruidoso.

This affiant further states that he never believed that Billy the Kid was killed by Sheriff Pat Garrett; that he heard from time to time throughout the years that Billy the Kid was still living.

This affiant further states that O.L. Roberts has the same blue-grey eyes, with brown spots in them; that his nose is straight, with high cheek bones, large ears, small feet and hands with large wrists, and he stands as straight as he stood in Lincoln County days; that he is still fast on the draw; that he talks and laughs the same, and looks the same in many ways; that he has no teeth now, and his hair is nearly gray with some dark streaks in it.

This affiant further states that he is of firm belief that Billy the Kid and O.L. Roberts are one and the same person.

SEVERO GALLEGOS
X (His Mark) (L. M. W.)
Affiant

Sworn to and subscribed to before me, a notary public, this 11th day of November, A. D. 1950.

[SEAL]   [s] LILLIE MAY WARD
Notary Public in and for Lincoln County, State of New Mexico.

STATE OF NEW MEXICO –ss.
County of Lincoln

Before me, the undersigned authority, a Notary Public, on this day personally appeared Mr. Severo Gallegos, known to me to be the person whose name is subscribed to the foregoing instrument and he acknowledged to me that he executed the same for the purposes and consideration therein expressed.

Given under my hand and seal of office this the 11th day of November, A. D. 1950.

[SEAL]
[s] LILLIE MAY WARD
Notary Public in and for Lincoln County, New Mexico
My commission expires, Feb. 5, 1953.

APPENDIX F:2

AFFIDAVIT OF MRS. MARTILE ABEL

STATE OF TEXAS –ss.
County of El Paso

Before me, the undersigned authority, a notary public, on this day, personally appeared Mrs. Martile Able, widow of John C. Able who died at the age of 56 years, in 1918, of the County of El Paso, and State of Texas, who upon her oath deposes and says:

That her name is Mrs. Martile Able, that she was born in Cook County, Texas, more than eighty years ago, that she was married to John C. Able, in Abilene, Texas, after which they moved to a Ranch on the Black River, south of Carlsbad, New Mexico, where they lived for about two years, Stonewall County, Texas; that years after which they moved back to Abilene, Texas; that they moved from Abilene to El Paso, Texas, about 1900, and she still resides in El Paso County, Texas.

This affiant further states that the family was well acquainted with Wm. H. Bonney, known as Billy the Kid; that Mr. John C. Able, the husband of this affiant, knew Wm. Bonney years before around Pecos, Texas, where the group of friends had a picture made in 1880, which picture is a good likeness of Wm. Bonney; that Wm. Bonney visited with the Able Family before, and after, the time it was said, Pat Garrett killed him in New Mexico; that John C. Able brought Wm. Bonney to their house on one day when he caught a, horse for Bonney to ride out; that this affiant cooked a meal that day that he ate in hiding; that Bonney rode away on the horse, that the horse came back home after Bonney made his journey; that the last time this affiant saw Wm. Bonney was about the year of 1902; that she did not see Wm. Bonney again until July 1, 1950, while he was visiting here in El Paso, at which time this affiant talked to Wm. Bonney about the old times around Pecos and other places; that he talks about the old times as we always knew them, that he laughs much the same, has the same keen blue eyes, long nose, large cars, small feet, small hands with unusually large wrists, stands and walks as straight as ever with a lively step, that he appears to be around ninety years of age, but appears much younger in general, with hair nearly gray, looks much the same only he is a little larger than when I last saw him in 1902; that he spoke about the times when John C. Able helped him and loaned money to him when he was on the dodge; that the pictures in his album from the time he was about 14, late twenties, fifties, eighties, and the present time show a marked resemblance to the old picture in our album made in 1880 at Pecos, Texas.

This affiant further states that it was generally known among friends that Billy the Kid was not killed by Garrett in New Mexico, like they said he was killed; that Billy escaped into Mexico; and that this affiant saw him after he came back to this country from Old Mexico.

This affiant further states that to the best of her knowledge, information, and belief Wm. H. Roberts, also known as Wm. H. Bonney, Billy the Kid, Texas Kid, Brushy Bill Roberts, O. L. Roberts is one and the same person as O.L. Roberts, who visited with us here during the first week of July, 1950, and further affiant says nothing.

[s] MRS. ABLE
Affiant

Sworn to and subscribed to before me, a notary public, this the 1st day of Aug., 1950 A. D.

[s] G. A. ARREDONDO
Notary Public in and for El Paso County, State of Texas.

STATE OF TEXAS -ss.
County of El Paso

Before me, the undersigned authority, a notary public, on this day personally appeared Mrs. Martile Able, known to me to be the person whose name is subscribed to the foregoing instrument and she acknowledged to me that she executed the same for the purposes and consideration therein expressed.

Given under my hand and seal of office this the 1st day of Aug. A. D. 1950.

[SEAL]
[S] G. A. ARREDONDO
Notary Public in and for El Paso County, State of Texas.
My commission expires, June 1, 1951

APPENDIX F:3

AFFIDAVIT OF JOSE B. MONTOYA

STATE OF NEW MEXICO -ss.
County of Lincoln

Before me, the undersigned authority, on this day, personally appeared Mr. Jose B. Montoya of Lincoln County, New Mexico, who, upon his oath, deposes and says:

That his name is Jose B. Montoya, that he was born on May 6, 187o, in Lincoln County, New Mexico, that his parents died when he was quite young, that he went to live with his sister, Mrs. Felicita Gabaro, and her husband, on a ranch in the Capitan Mountains, later moving to the Town of Lincoln where he went to school; that this affiant was well acquainted with Pat Garrett, John Poe, Sheriff Kimbrel, and most people in that country.

This affiant further states that he was well acquainted with Wm. Bonny, known later as the Kid, and Billy the Kid, that Bonny stayed, from time to time, at the home of this affiant in Capitan Mountains, and Lincoln Town, that he watched Billy the Kid target practice often, that he would throw quarters into the air while Billy the Kid would shoot them with his pistols; that Billy was a good shot, and fired pistols with either hand; that Billy the Kid was a small man with large ears, a long straight nose, big teeth, small feet, small hands with large wrists off of which he could slip handcuffs; that he stood as straight as an arrow, was a good dancer and singer; that the negro, George Washington played the guitar, and negro Bates played the fiddle; that Juan Patron was guard over Billy after Sheriff Kimbrel arrested him; that Sheriff Kimbrel was a friend of Billy; that Pat Garrett beat Sheriff Kimbrel in the election for Sheriff; that people said Sheriff Kimbrel was too friendly with Billy the Kid; that the Kid broke jail at Lincoln by killing the two guards, Olinger and Bell, escaping to Fort Sumner, N. M., where some people said Pat Garrett killed Billy the Kid, but many people did not believe that Garrett killed him; that the Kid escaped from Fort Sumner into Old Mexico.

This affiant further states that he did not believe the story of Garrett killing the Kid; that he and another man by the name of Green saw Billy the Kid at a bull fight in Juarez,

Mexico, in 1902, and both of them knew the Kid; that the Kid was well dressed, wearing a large hat and buckskin jacket, and was talking to two Mexican officers; that a man in El Paso told them later that the Kid had been in El Paso three times before; that this affiant did not see Billy the Kid again until talking with him today while he was visiting with Wm. V. Morrison and the Kid in Carrizozo, N. M.

This affiant further states that to the best of his knowledge, information and belief Pat Garrett did not kill Billy the Kid, because Billy the Kid had too many friends in that country, and for other reasons including the fact that this affiant saw Billy the Kid in 1902 at Juarez, and talked with him personally today; that Wm. Bonney, alias Billy the Kid, alias O.L. Roberts, is one and the same person as 0. L. Roberts; that he talks and laughs, looks much the same, only older than he did before.

[SEAL]
[s] Jose B. Montoya
Affiant

Sworn to and subscribed to before me, a Notary Public, this 3rd day of July, A. D. 1950.

[s] Otto E. Prehm
Notary Public in and for Lincoln County, State of New Mexico.

STATE OF NEW MEXICO –ss.
County of Lincoln

Before me, the undersigned authority, a Notary Public, on this day, personally appeared Mr. Jose B. Montoya, known to me to be the person whose name is subscribed to the foregoing instrument and he acknowledged to me that he executed the same for the purposes and consideration therein expressed.

Given under my hand and seal of office this the 3rd day of July, A. D. 1950.

[SEAL]
[s] Otro E. Prehm

Notary Public in and for Lincoln County, State of New Mexico.

My commission expires, February 13, 1951

APPENDIX F:4

AFFIDAVIT OF DEWITT TRAVIS

STATE OF TEXAS
County of Gregg

Before me, the undersigned authority, on this day, personally appeared Mr. Dewitt Travis, Longview, Texas, who, upon his oath deposes and says:

That his name is Dewitt Travis, that he is 63 years of age, that he was personally acquainted with Wm H. Roberts, also known as Wm. H. Bonney, "Kid," "Billy the Kid," Texas Kid, Hugo Kid, Brushy Bill Roberts, and O.L. Roberts, who died on December 27, 1950, at Hico, Hamilton County, Texas.

This affiant further states the following facts with reference to the above-mentioned Wm. H. Roberts:

I have known him all of my life, having been raised with him and being around him, more or less, since my early childhood. I knew him to be honest, upright, truthful, polite and mannerly. He did not use tobacco or alcoholics. He was not a large man. He stood about five feet and eight inches, weighing about one hundred and sixty-five in late years, standing as straight as an arrow, and walking with a brisk step all of his life without the use of a cane. He was fair complected with high cheek bones, long straight nose, large ears with the left ear protruding farther away from the head than the right ear, blue grey eyes keen and shifty, dark hair graying in late years, peculiarly shaped teeth with two large teeth protruding outward from under the upper lip and a large tusk on each side of his upper jaw, the teeth having been extracted in 1931 by Dr. Cruz, Gladewater, Texas. He had small feet and wore a size seven boot, small hands with unusually large wrists, well-shaped fingers and hands. He was a very muscular and well-built man, quick as lightning, calm and collected, ambidextrous but preferably left handed, quick on the draw, shooting a pistol with either or both hands, a good shot with a rifle, which he fired left handed. I have seen him shoot and I will say he was a very good shot. I have seen him in skirmishes in which he was level headed, calm and collected, never appearing nervous. He was a likeable fellow, always smiling and in good humor, looking much younger than he actually was in years.

He taught me to swim. It was during swimming in cold water that I noticed many scars on his body. He pointed out some of the scars, telling me how they were received. I remember a bullet scar about two inches in length across the top of his head a couple of inches from the forehead which he said was received in the gun battle with Garrett's posse in Fort Sumner, N. M., on the night of July 14, 1881, when Garrett made the claim of killing him. During this gun battle he also received a bullet in the left shoulder, which scar remained prominent. He had a scar about an inch long across the back of the right hand near the knuckle joints; a scar across the first knuckle on the forefinger (trigger finger) of the right hand; one scar inside on the kneecap of the left leg; two scars inside the shin near the lower part of the left leg and a bullet lodged in the muscle; one scar high up on the right hip received during the battle when Sheriff Brady was killed in Lincoln; and several other scars on his body.

His name was not O.L. Roberts, and he was not the son of the family in East Texas. They died thinking Bill was their son, but he was not. This happened in my lifetime, so I am sure of what I am saying. My father, Elbert Travis, and Brushy Bill's father, "Two-Gun Roberts" fought together in the Civil War. I have known him intimately all my life. He used different names at various times.

I do not recall the name he was using when he ranched in Old Mexico. He came back to Texas about 1884 and took the name the Hugo Kid while on the Anti-Horse Thief trail at Hugo, Oklahoma. He rode in the Wild West shows of Buffalo Bill and Pawnee Bill, later starting a Wild West show of his own. He ranched in Arkansas and Oklahoma in later years, moving to Gladewater, Texas, where he was well liked by everyone. Later on, he moved back to Hico, Hamilton County, in the community where he spent his childhood days. He would not admit that he was "Billy the Kid," New Mexican outlaw, until shortly before his death. But his intimate friends knew all the time that he actually was the New Mexican outlaw. I have seen him shoot and remove the hand cuffs from his hands like he did in the days of old.

The affiant further states that to the best of his knowledge, information, and belief the said Wm H. Roberts, alias Wm. H. Bonney, alias "Kid," alias "Billy the Kid," alias

Brushy Bill Roberts, alias O.L. Roberts are one and the same person. And that he was not killed by Sheriff Pat Garrett in Fort Sumner like they said he was killed in 1881, and further this affiant says nothing.

[S] DEWITT TRAVIS
Affiant
Sworn to and subscribed to before me, a notary public, this 12th day of December A. D. 1951.
[SEAL]
{s] MRS. ETHEL MARTIN
Notary Public in and for the County of Gregg, State of Texas

STATE OF TEXAS -ss.
County of Gregg

Before me, the undersigned authority, a Notary Public, on this day personally appeared Mr. Dewitt Travis, known to me to be the person whose name is subscribed to the foregoing instrument and acknowledged to me that he executed the same for the purposes and consideration therein expressed.

Given under my hand and seal of Office this the 12 day of Dec., A.D. 1951

[SEAL]

[s] MRS. ETHEL MARTIN
Notary Public in and for the County of Gregg, State of Texas
My commission expires, June 1, 1953

APPENDIX F:5

AFFIDAVIT OF ROBERT E. LEE

STATE OF LOUISIANA –ss.
Parish of E. Baton Rouge

Before me, the undersigned authority, a notary public, on this clay, personally appeared Mr. Robert E. Lee, of Baton Rouge, Parish of East Baton Rouge, State of Louisiana, who upon his oath deposes and says:

That his name is Robert E. Lee, that he is 76 years of age, that he was born near Corsicana, Texas, the son of James Lee of Virginia, that he was kidnapped by a band of horse thieves, and traders, at the age of 15 years, that, after being liberated from the band in the summer of 1889, he stayed at the ranch in New Mexico for a few months later drifting to "Scout's Rest Ranch," North Platte, Nebraska, which was owned by Colonel Wm F. Cody, known as Buffalo Bill; that Buffalo Bill hired this affiant at the ranch; that this affiant worked in Buffalo Bill's Wild West Show as body guard for Col. Cody; that Buffalo Bill's show was also known as "Congress of the Rough Riders of the World," with about six hundred people under his tent City outside the World's Fair Grounds at Chicago, Illinois, during the Exposition there in May, 1893.

This affiant further states that the first time he saw Wm. Bonney, alias the Kid, alias Billy the Kid, alias Texas Kid, was in the summer of 1889, at a ranch across the road from Fort Selden, New Mexico, when the Kid and his ranch pals rescued this affiant from the hand of thieves as they were camping at the ranch, doctoring their stallion; that the Kid was staying over at the ranch house; that William Bonney and his pals liberated this affiant at the ranch, and also disarmed the kidnappers then and there.

This affiant further states that it was generally known to him, and among friends of the Kid—some of whom were Buffalo Bill Cody, who hired the Kid in 1885, and subsequently; Pawnee Bill, or Major Gordon W. Lilly; T. B. Omohundro (Texas Jack) and Mexican Joe, both of whom worked with the Kid at Buffalo Bill's Place; Belle Starr; Indian Jim; Cherokee Bill; Ozark Jack; Miss Lou Mulhall; the James Brothers; John Trammel, who cooked for the Kid's father and his friends during the Civil War; Tex

Moore; and many other old timers—that Wm. Bonney was not killed by Pat Garrett and his deputies in 1881, as stated by hearsay for many years; that the Kid escaped from Ft. Sumner into Old Mexico where he lived with the Yaqui Indians in Sonora; that Billy the Kid assumed the name of the Texas Kid when he returned to this country from Old Mexico; that the Texas Kid worked in Texas, the Indian Territory, the Black Hills of Dakota, Idaho, and divers other places with intermittent trips back to Mexico, where he had ranches at different times, all of which facts were generally known to the Kid's friends.

This affiant further states that the Kid, New Mexican outlaw, was riding in Buffalo Bill's Wild West Show in Chicago, Illinois, in 1893; that the Kid was one of the best riders in the show; that the Kid obtained the name of Brushy Bill, the Scout, for his good work in the Anti-Horse Thief Association, sometime before the performance in Chicago in 1893; that Buffalo Bill fought Indians with the Kid's father; that Buffalo Bill was well acquainted with the mother of the Kid; that he hired the Kid because he was well acquainted with the pioneer Roberts family in Texas and wanted to help the Kid go straight.

This affiant further states that William H. Roberts, alias William H. Bonney, alias Kid, alias the Texas Kid, alias Brushy Bill Roberts, is a man who stands about five feet and eight inches, weighs about one hundred and sixty pounds, has dark hair, almost white at present, blue eyes with hazel spots in them, large ears, prominent straight nose, and high cheek bones; that the large crooked teeth are no longer in his mouth; that he has small feet, small shapely hands with large wrists; that he is a well-built man, standing and riding straight as an arrow, and walking with a lively step; that he is about ninety years of age but looks much younger; that he always appears in good humor, laughing quite a bit and smiling when he talks; that he has a soft and sort of high-pitched voice; that he was a good singer and dancer in his younger days; that lie is always friendly and has a lot of friends; that he is a man of good habits, refraining from the use of alcohol and tobacco, is well mannered and a nice man in general; that lie has a cool temperament, is steady nerved; that he is a good shot with a pistol with either hand, but preferably left handed; that he has a good record; that he has not been known to be in trouble since killing his two guards in his escape from the Lincoln County, New Mexico, jail in 1881.

This affiant further states that the last time he saw Wm. H. Roberts, alias Wm. H. Antrim, alias Wm. H. Bonney, alias Kid, alias Brushy Bill Roberts, alias O.L. Roberts, was at New York City in January, 1950. We both were there at the Jesse James Press Conference at that time.

This affiant further states that William Bonney was never shot and killed by Pat Garrett, or any other Garrett. No Sir, for I worked with him in the Colonel Cody Show, and I took orders to him from Colonel Cody. Don't you think Colonel Cody and I knew just who he was? Folks, I say take it or leave it, Billy the Kid is still riding, or the Kid will ride again. I know him just awful well. Many of the old timers said it was only hearsay that Pat Garrett killed Billy the Kid; that Wm. H. Roberts, alias Wm. H. Antrim, alias Wm. H. Bonney, alias Kid, alias Billy the Kid, alias Texas Kid, alias Brushy Bill Roberts, alias O.L. Roberts, the son of "Wild Henry" Roberts, is one and the same person as O.L. Roberts with whom I visited in New York City in January of 1950.

This affiant further states that to the best of his knowledge, information and belief the above-mentioned Billy the Kid was not killed by Pat Garrett at Maxwell's Home in Fort Sumner, New Mexico on July 14, 1881.

[s] ROBERT E. LEE
Affiant
Sworn to and subscribed to before me, a notary public, this the 5th day of July, A. D. 1950.

[SEAL]
[s] FLETCHER T. HINTON
Notary Public in and for Parish of East Baton Rouge, State of Louisiana.

STATE OF LOUISIANA
Parish of East Baton Rouge

Before me, the undersigned authority, a notary public, on this day, personally appeared Mr. Robert E. Lee, known to me to be the person whose name is subscribed to the foregoing instrument and he acknowledged to me that he executed the same for the purposes and consideration therein expressed.

Given under my hand and seal of office this the 5th day of July, A. D. 1950.

[s] FLETCHER T. HINTON
Notary Public in and for Parish of East Baton Rouge, State of Louisiana
My commission expires at death

ABOUT THE AUTHORS

C.L. SONNICHSEN

Charles Leland Sonnichsen received a Ph.D. from Harvard University and was a Benedict Professor of English at the University of Texas, El Paso. In addition to being a noted Southwestern historian and folklorist, he was a prolific author and screenwriter with several dozen books to his credit. Sonichsen was the 23rd president of the Western Historical Association.

WILLIAM V. MORRISON

William Vincent Morrison was born in Illinois to a prominent family descended from Lucien Bonaparte Maxwell. Mr. Morrison was a graduate lawyer, court appointed probate investigator, and genealogical researcher best known for his efforts in seeking a pardon for William H. "Brushy Bill" Roberts in 1950, a man who in the 1940s appeared claiming to be Billy the Kid. In addition to being widely respected for his character and legal work, Mr. Morrison was a member in good standing with the Missouri Historical Society. Mr. Morrison was also fluent in Spanish and was a popular lecturer in the Southwestern US and in Mexico.

THANK YOU FOR READING!

If you enjoyed this book, we would appreciate your customer review on your book seller's website or on Goodreads.

Also, we would like for you to know that you can find more great books like this one at www.CreativeTexts.com

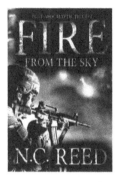

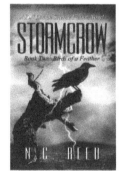

Printed in January 2025
by Rotomail Italia S.p.A., Vignate (MI) - Italy